Properties From Our Father

Seeing the Hand of God in Real Estate Transactions

LINDA R. ABRAMS

PRINTED IN THE UNITED STATES OF AMERICA

ISBN-10: 1490410163
ISBN-13: 978-1490410166

Library of Congress Control Number: 2013911206
CreateSpace Independent Publishing Platform
North Charleston, South Carolina

Table of Contents

To my dear friends

Minda Larsen & Ellen Good

Who, both in their nineties, often encouraged
me to complete this book

With Gratitude

*T*o my loving husband Keith who helped me "remember" as we traveled miles and miles of highway together while I wrote our stories.

To our children, Kristin & Paul, Tara & Mike, Joey & Nicole, Sean and Jacqui, who participated in sharing or allowed me to share their portions of our family story.

To my siblings, Ron Lutjens, Kurt Lutjens, Gary Lutjens, Glenn Lutjens and Kim Lutjens who helped me write *Chapter One* and graciously allowed me to share our Lutjens' family history.

To our patient and caring Realtors: Carol Chin, Carolyn Ragone, Chris & Dick Heck, Christian & Linda Lapense, Denise Johnson & business partner Barbara Scott, Gayle Billows, Joan Jacobs, John Stagliano, a realtor friend from whom we never bought or sold any properties, and Kathy Peters.

Westwood Avenue, River Vale, New Jersey

Chapter One

PROPERTY OF LOVE AND EQUITY

The House of Love

*I*t was about four AM and two men almost collided in the dimly lit hallway, both were overnight guests in the same house, but neither had met the other until that moment, on the way to the bathroom. And so, in their pajamas they made their introductions, each one inquiring of the other, "Who are you?" A few more hours and they would learn more about one another over morning coffee in the kitchen. Such awkward meetings were excusable if you knew the life style of my parents, Herman and Amy Lutjens. Their home was often bustling with people coming and going, like a bed and breakfast without the fees. But this moment was unique because generally my parents did their best to make introductions before retiring for the night.

Our Lutjens family legacy began in 1952 when my parents purchased an old house on seven acres of riverfront land, in River Vale, New Jersey, a suburban community, about 30 minutes from New York City. The house, originally a barn (circa 1850), had been converted after a devastating fire destroyed the original home in 1918. Without fire insurance, the only solution for the previous owners was to renovate their barn into a habitable home. The $15,000 our parents paid for the old house reflected its humble condition. Dad was very handy though, and room by room, year after year, he remodeled the ten-room, two bath house into a very warm and inviting home.

The kitchen was spacious with an eat-in nook large enough to seat eight. Long after my five siblings and I moved out, scores of people ate well in that kitchen. Festivities moved to the formal dining room with its long banquet table when the guests totaled nine or more. Over the years, Mom and Dad hosted a great many grand house parties, picnics, holiday meals, and family reunions. It truly was a festive place to visit—and live.

I remember the uneven floors. With few, if any level floors in the house, my youngest brother knew on which side of the table to position his electric football game to get the maximum downhill advantage. I would not call it cheating, but just a keen awareness of his surroundings.

As with most houses after each room is decorated, it was time to start all over again. Updating that beloved, charming, old house turned into a 50-year project for my parents.

Realizing the need for more livable space, Dad decided to create a family room out of the sun room (then considered a closed-in porch) at the front of the house. A business associate in Princeton, New Jersey allowed my father to dismantle part of his old barn. Dad used the hand-hewed beams and smoke grey barn siding to panel the entire room, including the ceiling. In that same space, he built a fireplace with red brick salvaged from the original home's cistern that he managed to find and dig up with the help of my two youngest brothers Gary and Glenn. The massive barn beam mantel adorned with holly and garland greens at Christmas is forever etched in my memory.

Not wanting to pay the price of a custom, oversized bay window for the adjacent garden room, Dad designed and built his own using one large picture window with double hung windows on both sides. My father was both creative and frugal. Off the garden room, Dad built a one-story redwood deck where he would sit after a hard day's work and appreciate the expansive view and beauty of his "estate."

The trees were old and magnificent: sugar maples, pines, red maples, shagbark, hickory and apple. In the summer those trees created a canopy of shade and in the fall, the brilliance of the leaves was breathtaking. On snowy winter days, we were living in a wonderland of white, snow-laden branches and pine needles. Though it was a magical place for children to grow up, one memorable winter day, the old house was in grave danger.

Post Christmas Fire

It was the day after Christmas and only minutes after lunch when the River Vale fire truck came screaming into our long circular driveway. Before our antiquated fire alarm let out its obnoxious wail, firemen were rushing into our house and up the stairs to douse the fire that one of my inquisitive little brothers started in the bedroom. He was playing with matches, lighting them one by one, blowing each one out and tossing the used matches on his bed. Unfortunately one of them wasn't totally extinguished and with the toss of that match, everything suddenly changed from calm to chaotic at the Lutjens' home.

Immediately, Mom had me gather my siblings to don our coats, hats, mittens and boots for a mini evacuation. The firemen arrived before we were all dressed and out the door, but within minutes I was able to walk us all through the snow to the safety of our neighbor's house.

Mom stayed back while the firemen were anxiously tossing the smoldering mattress from the second story window. They worked quickly to contain the fire so that it would not spread beyond that bedroom and, thankfully, it did not.

While all this activity was going on in the boy's bedroom, located on the second floor directly above the kitchen, Mom took one look at the just-abandoned table and spotted the mayonnaise jar and the ketchup bottle. She decided to clear away the condiments and tidy up the kitchen, because, as she later admitted, she was concerned what the firemen would think if they came down to announce that the fire was out, and saw that jar and bottle.

Bless her heart; Mom was a people-pleaser even when she did not need to be concerned. The firemen couldn't have cared less. Thankfully, the Lord spared our old house that day as His hand of protection allowed for the rapid response of the River Vale Volunteer Fire Department.

Our Big Family

I am the oldest of six children, with four biological younger brothers, Ron, Kurt, Gary and Glenn and an adopted Korean sister, Kim. In addition, we had many foster brothers and sisters who lived in our home over the years. They mostly came to us from Bergen County's Social Services Agency. A while back I counted them, but I can't quite remember if we had 30 foster children over a 20 year period of time, or 20 foster children over a 30 year period of time. Unfortunately we didn't keep a journal, but it was one or the other.

Our parents had a heart for troubled teens, and they demonstrated their care and concern by bringing them into our home and loving them. They led by example and taught us how to love and empathize with those less fortunate.

Mom and Dad also took in young women (mainly in their twenties) who came out of a type of half-way house, *The Walter Hoving Home*, affiliated with *Teen Challenge* in Garrison, NY. At the Hoving Home, the ladies began their spiritual journey to straighten out their lives. For some, the Lutjens' home became a safe place to begin their transition into a normal life. Amy and Hermie, as my parents were affectionately known, were available to help in any way possible.

The Gift of Hospitality

Share God's love with people who are in need. Practice hospitality.
Romans 12:13

After most of us were grown and out of the house, Mom and Dad continued to demonstrate their gift of hospitality by hosting refugee families, sponsored by their *Church of the Savior*, in Paramus, NJ. These courageous foreign visionaries were seeking political asylum in the United States to escape difficult circumstances of one kind or another in their home countries. They wound up on the receiving end of American hospitality—in our home—and political freedom, a freedom most continue to count precious to this day. Our home became an American haven to those seeking a life of safety and opportunity for themselves and their children. Families hosted came from Afghanistan, Bosnia, Cuba, Laos, and Poland—all found hope and love in my parent's home.

The following is an excerpt from a letter my parent's lawyer, David Rutherford, who also attended their church, wrote describing my parent's willingness to house these families:

"From time to time our congregation would decide to sponsor a refugee family, or an immigrant from a foreign land and in most cases there would be a need for housing. As many of us would nervously look around the room, wondering whether we could make such a commitment, or perhaps hoping to avoid it, Hermie and Amy never failed to willingly and joyfully raise their hands and open their home, sometimes for extended periods, to someone in need. I will never forget that. They were people of tremendous faith and commitment to their Lord."

Anointed with hospitable hearts, my parents were the hands and feet of Jesus to all who crossed their threshold. An entire book could be written about that special place, but for *Properties From Our Father*, River Vale is just the first chapter of my real estate experiences, and the beginning of a long and interesting journey.

Seven Acres Multiply

The residential portion of Dad's property occupied the front two acres, with our house sitting back off the road about 150-feet. Due to the large expanse of the front yard, a huge circular, gravel driveway marked the route from the south side of the property to the front door. In the spring, we would pass by bright yellow forsythia bushes on the right, and towering lilac bushes on the left, while catching a glimpse of the dogwood trees dotting the front yard. Azalea bushes were abundant, and most guest parking was in front of an old, 40-foot deep stone-lined well. No matter what the season, people were always commenting on the beauty of the property!

Soon after Dad and Mom signed the Contract to Purchase, they launched Lutjens Nursery and a landscaping business. Approximately four of the other five acres were designated for the nursery and a large vegetable garden.

With so many mouths to feed, my parents needed to grow a lot of their own produce. Dad grew up on a 40 acre farm in Hackensack, New Jersey, where cabbage, lettuce, potatoes, corn, carrots and more were raised. Working long hours on Grandpa's farm prepared Dad for success in growing plants, bushes and trees as well as vegetables for our personal use.

Though never trained in landscape architecture, Dad was creative with a natural ability to design. Eventually, he became a successful landscaper, known throughout the county for his talent, integrity, kindness, and humility. Many of the plants used on jobs came from his own nursery and what Dad didn't grow, he bought wholesale from other larger nurseries.

At the back of our property overlooking the Hackensack River, was wooded land that would later be portioned off into two conforming lots. As young children, we had great fun on the river—ice skating in the winter, and swimming and fishing on hot summer days. Little did my parents realize at the time how valuable those river lots would one day become.

> 'Improved land' (with water and sewer lines) is of greater value than 'raw land'

The New Development

When Dad began to think about his retirement, he didn't have a 401K, or an IRA. His wealth was in his family and his land.

During Dad's retirement transition my parents decided to sell the mid-section of the seven acres. All five unimproved lots were sold to a local builder for a total of $215,000. Wisely, that sale was made with the agreement that the Buyer would also improve the two river lots. Dad pursued this agreement with the builder because 'improved land' (with water and sewer lines) is of greater value than 'raw land.' Even with a new development of custom built homes centered in the middle of the original property, most of the old towering trees were still providing privacy and shade close to our house.

River Lots

The river lots were the second portion of the whole estate to be sold. Two brothers who owned a local diner approached my Dad about buying his riverfront lots. They each wanted to build a new house for their families side-by-side. A deal was made in the late seventies, and Dad sold those lots simultaneously for $245,000 each, without having to pay a real estate commission.

Mom and Dad retired on the front portion of the estate, a parcel close to two acres, with a little less than 200 linear feet along Westwood Avenue.

The Sub-division

By the time Dad was in his early eighties, he had to make the decision to sub-divide what was left of his land. Since our house had been positioned on the north side of the property and not centered, if a variance could be secured from the River Vale Zoning Board, it would be physically possible to sub-divide the one large lot into two conforming lots. Many years earlier, while in the process of selling his gladiola fields, a neighboring farmer thoughtfully offered Dad the opportunity to purchase 30 feet on the south side of our property. At the time, Dad's road frontage was short 33 feet, the amount necessary to ever be able to legally divide that portion of the land into two lots. That additional 30 feet would leave Dad only three feet short of what he would need in order to sub-divide. He would then have the option of applying for a variance when the time was right.

There is no doubt that my Dad had the future in mind, when he was prompted to get the necessary funds together to make that purchase. Often, it is human nature to think that we can delay important decisions without a worry about the future. However, it is prudent to be as prepared as Dad was because he wisely made that investment.

The wisdom of the prudent is to give thought to their ways.
Proverbs 14:8a

In the year 2002 our last two lots were sub-divided. The vacant lot on the south side of the property was sold to Dick and Chris Heck, real estate brokers, investors, and friends of our family. They built a beautiful, custom, 4,000-square-foot 'spec house,' which means that they did not have a buyer when building the house, but planned to market the property when the house was complete. The sale of that lot for $295,000 was transacted when the real estate market was on the rise. To our delight, the Heck's were careful to save as many of the mature trees as possible, allowing my parents to keep their beautiful property views.

Dementia Blessing

By the summer of 2003, it became clear that my parents could no longer live alone. Mom had a stroke in 2000 which resulted in a "vascular dementia" diagnosis. In 2003 Dad was diagnosed with a slow-growing type of lymphoma cancer. At age 85, Dad's short term memory was failing, and so neither parent was really able to help the other one. Previously we hired a trusted friend to live with my parents for a few years, but for Mom, no longer being able to manage her household became too great a challenge for everyone involved.

That August, after strong urging and support from my husband, Keith, the decision was made for Mom and Dad to move in with us in Delaware where we relocated the previous year. Dad knew in his heart that it was the right decision, but still didn't want to leave his beloved estate. The family agreed to rent the homestead for awhile so that leaving their home wouldn't feel so permanent to my parents. Thankfully, the declining mental state of my parents' minds actually made the transition easier. As painful as the developing dementia was for them and their loved ones, it was a blessing that their failing memories helped them to forget their loss.

On the day that I whisked my parents off to Delaware, we took only their clothes. It had been decided that my siblings would take care of cleaning out the house and Keith and I would be responsible for caring for my parents.

That day was as traumatic for me as it was for Mom and Dad. I couldn't cry because I didn't want to upset them, so I had to make small talk while trying not to think about what was happening. In my heart I knew they would never live there again, but I believe they were unaware that they would not return to their beloved home of 51 years.

Before we left, we helped our parents close this long chapter of their lives by walking through the whole house with them, sitting in each room and reminiscing, reading a passage of the Bible appropriate for that room, and then thanking God for His grace toward us all in that home. Finally, we commended Mom and Dad into the Lord's tender care for the new challenges that lay ahead. That experience brought closure for us all.

The Final Sale

Four months after my parents moved to Delaware, a one-year lease was signed by a tenant enamored with older homes. During the year that his home was rented, my Dad passed away at the age of 86. His end was peaceful and painless, for which we are most grateful. Herman Lutjens was truly one of God's saints; one to who people listened when he spoke and a man of incredible patience and wisdom.

After a period of time, the real estate market began to soften and tax considerations forced our decision to sell the final lot. The boom was clearly over and as builders began to cut back on spec homes, it was obvious that we needed to proceed with a listing to sell.

The value of the property was in the land, not the house. Hoping that an older home buff would be interested in preserving our homestead, we ran an ad in *This Old House Journal*, resulting in only a few non-serious inquiries. As time passed, we suspected a builder would be interested in purchasing that amazing lot to build a large upscale, new house, which is exactly what happened.

Months after we signed a listing agreement, a builder made us a low offer. Originally the asking price was $499,000. A short time later, we dropped the price by $20,000. When the Buyer's offer came in at $389,000, we were not impressed. However, since "time was of the essence" due to tax law, we did want to try to negotiate with someone who was at least willing to make an offer. Our family counter-offered with $449,000, which we felt was a fair price. The builder then countered at $399,000, obviously not much of an increase.

After much discussion with my siblings, we agreed to go back with our bottom line offer of $429,000, and kindly say, "We are done." It was thought that the (very old) house and the 'newer' three-car garage were worth only about $70,000. Taking our original asking price of $499,000, and subtracting the $70,000 value of the structures, in our minds, brought the value of the lot to $429,000. Our final counter offer was sent with a letter from me, reminding the Buyer of the beauty in the lot. I went on to explain that my Mother was in an expensive assisted living facility and the proceeds of that sale were to help pay for Mom's care.

I made it clear that if he was unwilling to come up $30,000 from his last offer, we would end negotiations, take our chances, and wait for another buyer. The Buyer responded by agreeing to our final number. That was a huge answer to prayer! The last corner of our property sold on time without a hitch.

Throughout this book I will refer to other letters that we have submitted during various real estate negotiations. Keith and I firmly believe that God has often used our transaction correspondence to accomplish His purposes. Realtors, as good and helpful as they are, often cannot pre-

> **A personal letter explaining one's position can make a big difference in whether or not a deal goes forward.**

cisely express their clients' thoughts as well as the client. While deals often seem to be very straight forward, they are not without the human element. It is people who interact and make decisions, even when representing institutions. A personal letter explaining one's position can make a big difference in whether or not a deal goes forward.

Over time, my parents reaped a rich harvest from their $15,000 purchase. God transformed that $15K investment in 1952, into well over a million dollars by 2007. These assets became their source of income during retirement years and especially in the declining years of their lives.

Mom and Dad had always been careful stewards of what had been entrusted to them. During those years of opening their hearts and home, the Lord was building equity in their land so that when they needed special care, there was more than enough money for their safety and comfort. The bountiful proceeds of the River Vale property would provide the means to hire caretakers for about nine years.

Our parents could not have known or even imagined that one day Mom's long term care would cost an average of $6,000 per month. Our family is forever grateful to the caretakers in St Louis who blessed our mother for five years of her life as a *Sunrise Assisted Living* resident.

> *A generous man will prosper; he who refreshes others,*
> *will himself be refreshed*
> Proverbs 11:25

Above all, my parents were blessed because of God's amazing grace. They taught us that our good works will not save us, but that we honor God and serve Him out of love for Him.

From my childhood home, through my real estate experiences as an adult, coupled with some stories described by our daughters, and in the final chapter, looking forward to that day when I cross from this life into the next, I share my heart, life and vision for eternity.

So many times over the years, the Lord has expressed Himself to us in the details of our real estate transactions. Dramatic situations occurred so often that these events could not have been coincidental. Not only was I able to conclude that there is a God in heaven who is concerned about the intricacies of our lives, but often He is orchestrating transactions on our behalf. Our responsibility is to walk so closely with Him that we can hear Him say, "This is the way, walk in it." Isaiah 30:21

Many verses in the Bible refer to homes and land. One of my favorites is:

> *"He determined the times set for them and the exact places*
> *where they should live."*
> Acts 17:26

How comforting to know that our God goes ahead of us and prepares homes for us to enjoy, and sometimes opportunities for investment. When we cannot imagine what He is doing, as everything seems to move so slowly, the Lord is busy, working behind the scenes, setting in motion His purposes for our lives.

"He sets all things in motion. In Him, and by His power, we live, move, and exist."
Acts 17:28

From idyllic River Vale, I moved 13 hours south of the border to a totally different world in Guadalajara, Mexico where my God-ordained story goes on.

RANCHO CONTENTO

Chapter Two

MEXICAN PROPERTY & FREE RENTAL

Rancho Contento

*A*fter completing a two-year tour-of-duty, serving as a medic with the U.S. Army in Japan, my first husband Tom, in his mid-twenties, decided that he wanted to pursue his long-time dream of becoming a surgeon. Tom's army experience confirmed his talent and destiny. Because of his 'ripe old age' of 27, he had to apply to medical schools outside of the United States. Within a year of beginning medical school at The Autonomous University of Guadalajara in Jalisco Mexico, Tom and I were married and I joined him in his Mexican adventure. It was 1974.

During those early years of marriage, we had very little money, partly because we were not getting any financial support from Tom's parents. And, except for a few rare exceptions, it was against Mexican law for Americans to work. We were living a very frugal existence on GI Bill student loans and the savings I had accumulated during our long engagement.

What was amazing was that, as poor as we were, we were able to live like we were wealthy. In the 70's when US dollars were exchanged for pesos, that money went a very long way.

After spending our first year of married life in an apartment in Guadalajara, we moved to a cozy villa on a golf course approximately one-half hour outside the city. The country club was known as *Rancho Contento*. Our rent was only $125 a month for a two bedroom, two bath California-style bungalow with a maid's quarters on a lovely lot adjacent to the ninth fairway of the golf course. From our living room we had a view across the fairway of the Clubhouse that had a large oval in-ground pool. This adorable villa had ceramic tile terracotta floors and a stucco fireplace flanked by sliding glass doors that led out to a patio, the focal point of our living/dining 'great room.' A plethora of roses, banana trees, rubber trees and bougainvilleas beautified the grounds, front and back.

To lower our living expenses, we housed a fellow medical student, a new friend of Tom's from New York City, in our guest bedroom. Having Mike live with us to help pay for the house also made it possible for me to have a maid (for only $4 a day, three days a week) and for Tom to have a gardener ($20 a month). Tom was able to study and play golf and I socialized with other medical student's wives and joined a local Mexican /American service sorority. It was a great life for a new bride, but not every day was tranquil.

One sunny summer day, we were on our way to take my sister Kim who had come for a visit, back to the airport. As we were passing through an intersection, the Mexican police began waving their hands in an unintelligible manner. Since we were in a hurry, and not wanting Kim to miss her plane, we ignored what we could not understand and kept driving. (In Mexico, encounters with the authorities can last for many hours.)

Within several minutes, an unmarked car passed us on the left with the policeman on the passenger's side aiming an M16 gun at Tom's head! In that moment, it became crystal clear they meant for us to pull over! Tom immediately responded to their dramatic request and by God's amazing grace, after we pretended not to speak any Spanish, within minutes they let us go.

I am not sure, but I believe it was because we had our newborn daughter, Kristin, with us in the car. The Mexican people really love babies and children. They consider their offspring to be their wealth We believe that God used our innocent baby to deter the Mexican police from their inexplicable mission. To this day we have no idea why they wanted us to stop. This is only one example of the various challenging situations we encountered during our Mexican journey.

Though we had our fair share of unusual circumstances often encountered in foreign countries, as newlyweds we were blessed to experience life in a different culture. Until 1977, when Tom had to return to the United States to complete his training, we were fortunate to live in that beautiful country club setting, and enjoy an amazing, un-anticipated lifestyle.

Though we felt very blessed while living in Guadalajara, one of our greatest joys came three years later when we made our final trip over the border and returned to the United States. We did feel like we wanted to kiss the ground because we were so happy to be moving back to our beloved Country. Many patriots agree that the experience of living on foreign soil helps one to better appreciate the United States of America.

Pregnant, Poor, and Prayerful

For your Father knows what you need before you ask Him.
Mathew 6:8

When we returned to the USA, Kristin was two years old and I was about seven months pregnant with our second daughter Tara. Because of my physical condition, job opportunities were scarce. Tom was about to begin his internship and we were still living on student loans, which amounted to about $400 per month, total, for living expenses. Of course that amount of money went a lot further in the late 70's than it does today, but in New Jersey, one of the most expensive states, there were no decent rentals for anything close to what we paid in Mexico.

I knew when we were about to leave that Country, my life of luxury in the aptly named *Rancho Contento* was about to take a major turn. Housekeepers and gardeners would be totally out of the question for many years to come. Nevertheless, I was anxious to return to family and friends and for Tom to continue his intern-ship training where he had been accepted in an American hospital at the Jersey Shore.

After analyzing our financial situation, I realized we would have to begin to seek a *rent-free* place to live. It seemed like a wild idea, but I was confident that God knew our needs, and would supply from His abundance.

My idea was to try to get a job as superintendents of a garden apartment complex, where, in exchange for a free apartment, I could collect the rent payments and Tom could handle light maintenance. Anyone who knows anything about this type of 'job' will agree on just how naïve I was. It was only later in life, when I became the landlord, that I would find out just how much work is involved in managing tenants.

In early June, 1977, Kristin and I were staying with my parents in River Vale while Tom was wrapping things up in Mexico and pre-paring to drive back with our personal belongings. His internship would not begin until August 1, at the *Jersey Shore Medical Center*, in Neptune, NJ. My father-in-law, who also lived in Jersey offered, in Tom's absence, to drive me from Bergen County down to Monmouth County to look for housing in preparation for my husband's return.

Our goal was to check out any potential rentals in garden apart-ment complexes near the hospital and specifically seek out a super-intendent's job. The most reasonable two bedroom apartment that we could find rented for $350 per month and there were no super-intendent jobs anywhere. Though discouraged, I still believed that we needed to continue to ask the Lord for a *free* place to live. My idea didn't seem to be panning out, and I had no idea how the Lord would answer my request, but God knew that we could not afford to spend almost our whole monthly allowance on rent.

Upon returning to River Vale, Mom asked me if we found anything suitable. When I explained that we had not, she asked me if I wanted to sit down and pray with her. My parents were real 'prayer warriors' who prayed about everything. They considered no matter too small for God's concern. While growing up, whenever we would come to them with any challenge, the first question they would ask was simply, "Did you pray about it?" We soon learned that it was pointless to ask them for input until *after* we had prayed. They taught us that prayer not only changes things, but that it will also provide clarity and direction.

> **No matter is too small for God's concern.**
>
> **Prayer not only changes things, it will also provide clarity and direction.**

Call to me and I will answer you and tell you great and unsearchable things you do not know.
Jeremiah 33:3

Forever I will be grateful that the Lord blessed me with parents who had such an intimate relationship with Him. They were powerfully influential in shaping my faith-walk with the Lord. Educating our children about God and His incredible love for us is the best legacy that parents can leave. Teaching those young, impressionable hearts and minds, how to walk with the Lord far outweighs anything else that we can give them, including an Ivy League education. Mom and Dad truly set a godly example for me and all my siblings.

That afternoon Mom and I sat down at the kitchen table and prayed together, repeating our request for *rent-free* housing. We reminded the Lord that our need was great, and our finances minimal. Our focus was on a verse in Jeremiah:

For I know the plans I have for you says the Lord,
plans to give you a hope and a future.
Jeremiah 29:11

As soon as we lifted our heads, Mom said, "You know, there is a couple at our church, who have a summer home at the shore. Would you like me to call them and see if they ever rent out their house in the winter? If they do, maybe if I explain your circumstances they might give you a highly reduced rate."

I agreed, but knew that we could not afford even a winter rental at the Jersey Shore. It certainly would not hurt to make the call. I reasoned that maybe because we had just prayed, Mom was being motivated by the Holy Spirit. At that point, we did not even know if their property was anywhere near the hospital where Tom would be working.

> I believe that educating our children about God and His incredible love for us is the best legacy that parents can leave

Mom picked up the phone and called the Meier's and Jim Meier answered the phone. Mom went into a whole dissertation on the 'state of our lives,' explaining that I was about to have a baby; that we were just returning to the US after three years in Mexico and that we were living on student loans. By the time she finished, while listening to her describe my total situation, I was beginning to feel depressed for myself! Jim responded by saying, "Hold on a minute, let me talk to Alice."

God's Rapid Response

A few minutes later, Jim returned to the phone and said to Mom, "We would love to have Linda and her family stay in our house at the shore. The house is in Brick Township, about 14 miles from the Medical Center, so it wouldn't be too far away for Tom. We often thought about renting it in the winter," he continued, "but never wanted to trust strangers with our home. It would give us peace of mind to have Linda and her family there."

Mom asked how much rent they would need to charge us. Jim responded, "We would *not* charge them *any* rent, they would only need to pay for the utilities."

Mom couldn't thank Jim enough and when she hung up, we both returned to prayer, praising the Lord for answering so dramatically and graciously. We prayed for a *free* place to live and God honored our prayers, not because we are good, but because He is good. He answered within minutes of that prayer session and we did not forget to thank Him. I could hardly wait to tell Tom.

But there was another blessing coming.

The next day, Alice called me back and asked where we would live for the summer since we couldn't have their shore home until Labor Day. I told her that we could stay at my parents and in August when Tom would begin his program, he would have to commute the 75 mile distance to the hospital, alternating nights with sleeping in the doctor's lounge. Alice then suggested, "Why don't you and Tom house-sit here in our home in Paramus while we are at the Shore? Then on Labor Day, we will just switch houses."

> The Lord's provision for us is always so much better than what we could ever imagine for ourselves

Wow! The Meier's primary residence was a five-bedroom, three-bath, two-story colonial with central air. The shore house, which we would take over in September, was a three bedroom, one bath ranch in Brick Township, on a lagoon with a dock. What a difference between those two wonderful houses that God had planned for us, and the small garden apartment that I had originally envisioned.

For my thoughts are not your thoughts,
neither are your ways my ways, declares the Lord.
Isaiah 55:8

The Lord's provision for us is always so much better than what we could ever imagine for ourselves. We lived in that waterfront house for two winters. Once Tom started his surgical residency program, he began to receive a pay check and thankfully, we were eventually able to move into cost-effective hospital housing.

Unfortunately, it didn't take long for our marriage to enter the danger zone. We would end up spending more time apart than together during Tom's five years in the residency program at Monmouth Medical Center in Long Branch, NJ.

THE CAPE COD

Chapter Three

MY SETTLEMENT PROPERTY

Encore!

I n 1980, while separated from Tom and working as a marketing representative for a wholesale seafood company, my entrepreneurial spirit kicked in and I decided to open an upscale consignment boutique. Most of my adult life, I have been an avid consignment shopper. A combination of financial constraints during my marital separation, the thrill of the hunt for a great bargain and a vision for a classy consignment shop, influenced my decision.

Regardless of our income levels over time, I still enjoy consignment shops of all kinds. In recent years these shops have become more sophisticated, but it wasn't always that way. In the late 1970's when I had to shop in resale shops out of necessity, most were unappealing in every way. They had the thrift shop feel of dingy décor, poor quality, and lack of order. They were mostly patronized by those of us who could not afford to shop in retail stores. The decorator in me dreamed of an upscale consignment shop. I believed that *if* such a shop was created, the people would come. The idea began to stir within me, and I gave serious and prayerful consideration to opening that kind of a place.

After the promise from Tom to co-sign a $10,000 loan, and confirming my eligibility with the bank, I began the search for a store front. By that time, I knew enough about the importance of location in real estate, so it was crucial to find a main street address. I did find the perfect space for my shop, located on the corner of Main Street and 9th Avenue in Belmar, NJ, a desirable, seaside, resort town. My front door would be steps away from the bus stop and only hundreds of feet from the local supermarket. The sign read, *Encore*, with the tag line, *A Unique Consignment Shop*.

Finding that perfect location motivated me to take a leap of faith and go forward with my idea. The 1100-square-foot store had been prepared for me by the previous tenant with wall-to-wall carpeting—an essential element in my vision for the shop. My brother Gary came down to the Shore with my Dad and together, they built wall racks for the clothes, along with dressing rooms. A previously owned, executive cherry desk and standing floor racks were purchased from liquidation sales.

The desk was my check-out area and I opted to use a cash box in the top drawer in lieu of an unsightly register. A decorative lamp for the desk and a pretty brass chandelier added a warm glow to the unattractive florescent lighting. Large paned windows expanded from across the front of the store and around to the side of the building where I also had good exposure. Raised platforms were in place for the inexpensive mannequins displayed in the window areas. Lattice was hung in the side window as a back drop for clothes that could be easily displayed. With the preparation work complete, we had created one of the first classy consignment shops at the Jersey Shore.

Advertisements in the local newspapers for quality, gently used clothing, got results and consignors started to call for appointments to bring in their unwanted items. I took men's and women's clothes and maintained rigid standards of quality. Everything had to be spotless, dry-cleaned or washed, pressed and on hangers. The resort town location drew customers from many states, especially during the summer season. In a short period of time, *Encore* earned a reputation of being one of the nicest consignment shops in the region.

The store was so upscale that people who did not read the sign sometimes were unaware that the clothing wasn't new, until they realized that there was only one of everything. Occasionally someone would remark that they would never buy *used* clothes. I would gently remind them that when they patronize hotels they sleep in *used* sheets. To that remark they never knew how to respond.

The people did come, and to my accountant's surprise, I started to show a profit after only three months in the business. He said that most small businesses take a lot longer to get up and running and often do not show any profit the first year.

Thankfully, the Lord brought me through some pre-decision jitters via unusual encouragement. For readers who have an entrepreneurial spirit, but have been held back by fear, I want to share the catalyst that confirmed my decision to step out in faith.

The day before I was to sign and submit my *Encore* lease to the landlord, I was starting to get nervous and began to second-guess my decision to go forward with my dream shop. It was a big step for a single mom with two children to take on a loan for

> "I taught my sons to never be afraid of failure for following the American Dream"

a start-up business. The statistics for start-up companies were not in my favor. I began to question whether or not God wanted me to go through with everything. I still had a small window of time to back out of the deal by simply giving the $10,000 back to the bank. Once I signed the lease, I knew I would be truly committed.

That next morning, when I was scheduled to submit my lease with the security deposit, a TV daily show featured a story about a sheep herder. After emigrating from another country with his family to the United States, he settled out west where he was running a very successful shepherding enterprise. The man made a statement in the interview that 'spoke' directly to me, and I will never forget it.

He said, "I taught my sons to never be afraid of failure for following the American Dream." Immediately I realized that God was using that TV program (which I hardly ever watched) to encourage me to take the risk to go forward with *Encore*. I did sign those papers that day, and ultimately the Lord bountifully blessed *Encore*. Years later I would sell the business to Richard (my banker across the street) and his wife, Mary Sherman, who continued to successfully serve the community with affordable clothing for another 14 years before retiring.

Our Unfortunate Divorce

By 1985, Tom finished his surgical residency and began his private practice. In one more attempt to see if we could salvage our marriage, we were reconciled after our longest separation of nine months and rented a property in the quaint seashore town of Avon, New Jersey. Originally, the house had been designed with a physician's office attached. It was the perfect place to begin the practice, enabling us to keep overhead expenses low. This was the only house near enough to the hospital that included a former doctor's office in the floor plan. That charming Cape Cod home was another example of God's thoughtful provision for our family.

Unfortunately, those many years of surgical training took a major toll on our marriage. Tom was in a world completely separate from mine. He was part of a health care system that required long hours day and night and soon, his hospital co-workers became his family. Sadly, within the first year of his residency program, Tom decided that he did not want to be married any more. Initially, I was devastated and wanted desperately for God to heal our marriage, especially for the sake of our daughters. And, we did struggle through multiple separations and feeble attempts to reconcile. Over time my commitment to Tom waned as well and in January of 1988 we divorced, but not before Tom made sure to provide a permanent roof over our heads.

In 1985 housing prices started to rise, and Tom and I started looking for a house to purchase as it was no longer prudent to rent. With a year of private practice as a vascular surgeon behind him, Tom was able to qualify for a Veteran's Administration mortgage. After supporting Tom through medical school and residency, we both felt that the girls and I deserved the security to live in a house that we owned. I told Tom *before* we started looking for a house that my plan was to file for a divorce *after* the purchase. Not wanting to be accused of being deceitful in any way, I was honest about my intentions.

We looked for a modest home big enough for the girls, me and a few guests, who would come to the Shore for visits. Tom was generous. He began taking care of us with the purchase of an adorable Cape Cod-style house in Neptune, New Jersey, which would soon become my settlement property.

The four-bedroom, two-and-a-half-bath Cape, with a finished basement and an in-ground pool, was perfect for Kristin, Tara and me. It was listed at $108,900, but the listing was soon to expire. The agent told us that the Sellers were planning to raise the price when relisting the house. We were able to make our full price offer ten days before the six month expiration date and the deal was executed. About 18 months after we moved in, our divorce was final. The girls and I spent quality time in that cute house as we worked together to rebuild our lives.

Affordable Interiors by Kristalyn

While having fun decorating my charming Cape, I was reminded that I had talent in that field. Before I married Tom, I had worked for several firms designing kitchens and bathrooms. My Associate of Arts degree prepared me more for life than for a career, however, after a year in retail management, I was offered an on-the-job training position with a friend of my parents who owned an upscale kitchen design firm, the Jay L. Whittaker Co. That was an amazing opportunity.

I soon discovered that designing beautiful and practical kitchens and baths brought me great satisfaction. When Jay's daughter finished college, and wanted to work for her Dad, I agreed to leave, because he could not use both of us. Within a few weeks, I was able to find a similar position with the Ken Bauer Company in Hillsdale, New Jersey, where I worked as a design consultant until I married and moved to Mexico.

The nice thing about the decorating industry is that in most states, you do not need a license or a degree to get started. Being a decorator is like being an artist with a God-given gift. One has to be able to envision ideas that cannot be seen except in their mind's eye. These many years later, as the décor in my Cape house evolved, I thought it might be wise to use my talents and start a decorating company that would market to middle income clients.

As a result of my lucrative divorce settlement, I had enough money to comfortably pay all my bills however; I didn't have extra money to start a company. I did know that if it was God's will for me to own a decorating company He would surely provide the necessary funds. Within months that is exactly what He did.

While visiting my parents in North Jersey, a neighbor friend was invited to join us for dinner. Towards the end of her visit, she asked me what I was going to do with my life now that I was divorced. With the girls in school all day, I was blessed with time to pursue my interests. The desire to be and feel productive has always been a deeply-rooted need of mine. I told Mom's friend that I was prayerfully considering starting my own interior decorating company.

She queried, "How much money do you think you will need to make that happen?"

I told her that I was estimating about $4,000 since my plan was to work the business from home.

Our friend's immediate response was, "I will give you a $4,000 loan if you decide to go forward." It was that simple. One minute I am sharing an idea that has been on my mind, and the next minute God moved on our friend's heart to offer me a loan for the entire amount. Needless to say, I felt that such a generous offer was confirmation that I should go ahead and launch a decorating company. Within a month, *Affordable Interiors by Kristalyn* became a reality. (KRIS-TA-LYN was derived from the first syllables of my two daughter's names, Kristin and Tara and mine.) Once again I was able to see the hand of God working on my behalf. The loan was repaid in a timely manner and then, as if that wasn't enough, God opened another unexpected door of opportunity.

While shopping for a client at *Color Tile* in Eatontown one afternoon, the manager, Larry, began chatting with me and soon found out that I was a decorator. In the course of the conversation, we also found out that we were both Christians. When Larry heard that I was working *Affordable Interiors* from home, he asked if I might be interested in moving my desk and phone to his showroom without any cost to me.

In exchange for the complimentary space, Larry wanted me to help his customers whenever they requested help from a decorator. Larry's proposal was that, when *Color Tile* customers were shopping in the store, I would help them with no charge to them or *Color Tile*. If, however, they wanted an in-home consultation, they would pay me directly for that service and consequently become one of my clients. As soon as Larry got permission from *Color Tile* senior management, I moved into the large showroom and *Affordable Interiors* grew even faster.

When finalized, this new arrangement was even further affirmation from the Lord that I was in His will. I walked into *Color Tile* thinking I was simply going to pick up tile samples for a client, and an hour later, walked away with the offer of a rent-free 10x10-square-foot space to grow my business. What an awesome God we serve! He is often dramatic, blessing us when we are not even looking.

My New Husband

Because I was a relatively young divorcee, my hope was that one day I would be able to remarry and get a second chance at finding a husband to last a lifetime. Eventually, a blind date arranged by mutual friends would be my initial encounter with the man to whom I am now happily married. It took us a while to figure out that we were meant for each other, but after years of prayer and contemplation, Keith Abrams and I began to make plans to get married. In addition to a wonderful husband, the Lord also blessed me with two loving step-children, Sean Keith and Jacqui Elaine Abrams. Thankfully, we serve a God of second chances. While the Bible does say that the Lord "hates divorce"

> **Thankfully, we serve a God of second chances**

(Malachi 2:16), He also is a forgiving God and the Bible never refers to divorce as the unforgiveable sin. After many hours of counseling, I finally did feel ready to marry again.

Family Blending

Unfortunately, it was more challenging than I imagined it would be for my teenage daughters to accept a new step-father moving into the home that the three of us had shared for years. While I tried to be a good mother and wife during the post-wedding transition period, looking back, I feel that I failed my children by not being able to comprehend their emotional pain. Kristin and Tara were struggling with a mother who was expecting them to embrace their step-father with open arms. Keith had been so good to all of us; I could not begin to understand the girl's resistance to him.

In hindsight I see more clearly from their perspective. I now believe divorced parents need to approach such situations with gentle understanding of the challenges that step-children, especially teens, face when being forced to "get with the plan" that is totally out of their control or ability to influence. I was expecting my children to be happy for me. What I could not understand was how broken and hopeless they were feeling. Though their Dad had remarried several years before me, my remarriage doubly cemented the fact that their biological parents would never be together again.

It seems to me that children of divorce often have a nagging false sense of hope for their parents to reconcile. After becoming more aware of their pain, I have since apologized to Kristin and Tara who have graciously forgiven me. Thankfully their relationship to Keith has improved dramatically in the past 20 years. It is by God's grace that my husband and children continue to work at strengthening their relationships with each other. Family harmony is important to each of us. While none of our relationships are perfect, we all continue to trust the Lord to empower us to love one another more and more. Love is much more of a decision than it is a feeling. Thankfully, we all have *chosen* love.

Our Adopted Son

While in the middle of my divorce from Tom, I met a 12-year-old boy from our church whose father had passed away and his mother Bonnie was in the hospital. One day I was asked to pick up Dominick Joseph Pagano after school and drive him to the home of the lady who was keeping him overnight until Bonnie could return home. This young man was so impressive because he was polite, intelligent and sweet. On the way to our destination, I asked Joey (his nickname) lots of questions about his life. Knowing that his mom had many life-challenges including financial instability, I needed to be certain that Joey was not involved with drugs of any kind before I would invite him to my home. At the time Kristin was 13 and Tara was 11 years old so I needed to be careful for their safety. He assured me that he was not involved with anything ugly like drugs.

Shortly after we met, I began to invite Joey and his mother and sister for holiday gatherings as they had no other family. I hosted some birthday parties for him, and simply began to treat Joey like a son. When Keith and I began a serious relationship, he and Joey started to bond.

One Father's Day, years after we were married, Joey came over for a barbeque and took Keith aside (by this time he was 26 years old) to tell Keith that he thought of him like a father. By that time, Keith loved Joey like a son, and after that day, we decided that we wanted to "adopt" Joey in the Biblical sense. He was too old to adopt legally, but after having one-on-one conversations with our biological children and getting their blessing, we added Dominick Joseph Pagano to our Wills, and have made him an equal heir to whatever estate we will have to leave to our children.

Now, when people ask us how many children we have, we say that, "Between us we have five." Keith and I both love Joey as one of our own and feel blessed by his presence in our family. We have great respect and admiration for our biological children, Kristin, Sean, Tara and Jacqui who welcomed Joey into our family with open arms and unselfishly are willing to share their inheritance. Joey is now married to his lovely wife Nicole and has a young son, Dominick Junior.

Decision to Sell

Initially it was our goal to live in the Cape Cod house in Neptune, NJ, until both girls graduated from high school. However, after we were married about six months, it seemed that it might be better to sell my house and buy something together so that we could have an 'our house.' Kristin was about to leave for *Taylor University* in Indiana and Tara was a junior at our local Christian high school. We were free to move to multiple towns as long as they were within driving distance of the high school.

Our Cape house was sold in about 30 days as I recall, and the closing was scheduled for mid-January. Both Kristin and Tara struggled with the changes that were imminent, but as a couple, and after prayerful consideration, Keith and I knew it was the best thing for us to do for our family.

It was also clear that my house was too small for all four of us. Sometimes parents have to make some very difficult choices. With a firm contract in hand from the quick sale of the Neptune house, we were able to begin a serious search for a home that would have both of our names on the new deed.

THE CUSTOM RANCH

Chapter Four

*Y*ears before we met, Keith worked extensively with the mother of Sean's high school friend searching for a house. Carol Chin from the Harry Lane Agency had shown Keith numerous properties, but it never seemed to be part of God's plan for Keith to make a purchase. Out of loyalty to Carol, we chose her to help us find our next home. Sometimes it is in looking back that we can see why things happened as they did. Ultimately, owning only one property between us really simplified our lives when we got married.

As I recall, there wasn't a lot of inventory on the market at that time, but I was determined to find a house with some charm. Keith and I have always been enamored by the ambiance of older homes, however, at that time in our lives we were open to anything the Lord might have in mind for us. Again, since Tara was in a private school, we were free to live in any town of our choice that was reasonably located for easy carpooling.

We toured many homes with Carol and finally found the right one, but charming is not how I would describe it. The last house in our price range to be previewed was a custom ranch in Wall Township, NJ and the price had just been reduced by $20,000. Before we took the tour, Keith advised Carol to meet us at the house with contracts, as he was quite certain that, after reviewing the listing, we would likely be making an offer. Since the Neptune house was already under contract and "time was of the essence," we realized that we would likely have to make some concessions on our wish list.

This custom-built ranch with three bedrooms and two baths (one pink and the other bright yellow), had cream walls and taupe carpeting in every room. The good news was that the house was solid and we could live with the color scheme until we had the money to make changes. The pluses of the house included an open sunken family room off the kitchen, a finished basement, an attached garage and an in-ground swimming pool on an expansive, beautiful lot.

The asking price was down to $209,000. Keith decided we would offer $180,000 because the house had been on the market for such a long time. (I am confident that the Lord had been saving that house just for us.) Keith was also expecting the owners might respond with a counter offer and he wanted some wiggle room to negotiate.

During the tour, we noticed numerous religious plaques and an open Bible, leading us to believe that the Sellers, Mr. and Mrs. Barber, might be Christians. When we made our offer, Mr. Gene Barber, was on a business trip, making it necessary to wait for his return before he would sign off on his response. He and his wife asked us to up our offer a little more but didn't give us a figure. We raised our offer to $182,000 and we had a deal.

Though we had not yet met in person, I immediately sent the Barbers a *Thank You* note for their willingness to sell to us. I explained that we had prayed for a long time that the Lord would lead us to the right house for our family and that we had a real peace in our hearts that their house was the right choice. Knowing the Barbers were the original owners, who made many memories under that roof, I thought they would appreciate any efforts on our part to preserve their home.

Prior to the closing, Keith's parents were up from Virginia for a visit. We wanted them to be able to see the house, so we asked Carol to arrange with the Barbers another house tour. They agreed to be available right after church on Sunday morning.

Mr. Barber came to the door when I rang the bell and as soon as we looked at each other, we realized we knew each other from a church I had attended several years before. I had not recognized his name on the *Contract to Purchase* because, on legal documents, he used his full name, Elvis Eugene Barber. I knew him only as Gene. And Gene didn't recognize my name on the contract because, since I had last seen him at a prayer meeting several years before, I remarried and had a new last name.

Both of us stood in amazement as we realized that we had put together a God-ordained contract without realizing who all the players were. As attendees of those prayer meetings for almost a year, Gene and I knew one another fairly well.

Not only were the Barbers gracious enough to allow us another tour with Keith's parents, but when we walked in the dining room the table was already set for a Sunday brunch. The Barbers wanted to have time to give us details about the house, contractors, etc., before the closing so they prepared delicious treats for us.

During that time of warm fellowship, Gene explained that after he received our *Thank You* note he was excited to share the note with his friends at the church. Gene told us that when they put the house on the market, he and all his prayer partners prayed that Christians would buy their house. Our note was confirmation for the Barbers that they made the right decision in agreeing to sell to us. Seeing Gene face-to-face was our confirmation that we chose the house that God had in mind for us.

While initially the house didn't have all the charm I was looking for, it did offer lots of potential and I was able to work my craft and add some drama. Needless to say, we changed the color schemes in every room.

Some of our changes included the transformation of our foyer with a faux-painted dramatic white-on-white technique. White fluted columns installed between the living and dining areas highlighted a distinct separation of the space. For symmetry and light, we added another window to the master bedroom and in the master bath creamy stone tiles replaced the bright pink 70's tile. Positive changes were made over time as little by little the house developed character.

The Sound of Gushing Water

Early one morning I abruptly awoke to what sounded like someone taking a shower with the door open in the main bathroom of our house. Keith was still in bed and no one else was living with us at the time. Feeling apprehensive, I woke Keith and rushed towards the bathroom down the hallway, only to discover that water was gushing everywhere from the washing machine hose in the adjacent laundry room.

> **Safety Tip:**
>
> *The life expectancy of a wash machine hose is 5-7 years. Install a metal hose – it will not burst. And, install a valve that can easily shut-off water completely between washings.*

Judging from the flooded scene surrounding me, I determined that the hose likely burst sometime in the middle of the night. At least one inch of water lay on the kitchen floor and was seeping into the family room, dining room and hallway.

The greatest damage was done to the finished basement, which, by that time was drenched in about four inches of water. All the carpeting, paneling and computers (my office was in the basement) were destroyed. In addition, Keith's 60's album collection valued at $1400 was ruined. When the claim had been adjusted, the insurance company sent us a check for a little over $12,000.

We had no idea that the life expectancy of a wash machine hose is only five-to-seven years. We also did not know that you can install a metal hose that will not burst, along with a valve that can easily shut the water completely off between washings. This practical information could have saved us from the terrible mess and losses that we sustained. Unfortunately, we learned all this *after* the flood.

The silver lining in that dark cloud was that we were able to use the insurance money to finish updating our home. The following year, the renovations were complete and the house was ready for the market. While the proceeds from the flood insurance blessed us with funds to complete our decorating projects, the devastation one feels during such an ordeal hardly seems worth the money for the repairs.

Unfortunately, when it was time for our annual homeowner renewal, our insurance company canceled our policy. Thankfully our friend and agent, Phil recommended a company who accepted us but charged a little higher rate. At that point, we were grateful to be able to purchase another home owner's policy, even if it was more costly.

Should We Sell?

We were empty nesters in a moderate sized home, with an unused in-ground pool that was ingesting expensive chemicals. After five years living in Wall Township, we thought that it might be the right time to sell our newly updated home while it still looked fresh. It was important to determine *if* it was God's plan for us to sell. Sometimes one of the ways that we are able to discern God's will for our lives is to 'test the waters' (while praying diligently) and see how the circumstances unfold.

In January of 1998, Keith and I decided to put 'the ranch' up for sale through Labor Day. We reasoned that if our house didn't sell during our time frame, we would take it off the market and stay put for a while longer. Initially we did not list with a realtor. Because we had minimal equity in the house, we decided to try to market the house ourselves. In April, we hosted several Open Houses resulting in average attendance and no offers.

It had always been our intention to work with any realtor who might bring us a buyer. A realtor is worthy of a commission because they have greater access to serious buyers. In addition, a real estate agent is extremely helpful throughout the sales process. They handle all the paperwork and inspections. With only a few exceptions, Keith and I buy and sell real estate with the help of competent realtors.

One evening, a realtor called us while we were having dinner to announce that she had an offer to present and wanted to come right over to meet with us. Earlier that week, we had been negotiating a contract on an income property located in the seaside resort town of Belmar, New Jersey, on Briarwood Road, which I talk about in *Chapter Seven*. One of the self-imposed conditions of our offer for the Belmar property was that we have a lease for at least one unit within a specified time frame. The time had just expired and we did not yet have a lease.

Before dinner that same evening, Keith composed an email to the Briarwood realtors indicating that we had not met our own criteria and would likely have to walk away from the purchase, but Keith decided to wait until after dinner and one more discussion with me, before pushing the "Send" button. Walking away from the Belmar property was a very difficult decision because we really believed that the duplex was the perfect income property for us.

While we enjoyed our meal, the email sat waiting on the computer. The timing of the realtor's call with an offer on our ranch could not have been more perfect. While I don't remember the exact numbers, the offer she brought us was very fair and we signed the contract immediately.

Now that we had a signed agreement for our personal residence, *we* became the qualified tenants for the income property in Belmar and would be able to proceed with its purchase. We sat stunned by how the Lord blessed us with a sale on our house less than an hour before backing out of the purchase of the Belmar property.

A week later, however, our Buyers had to back out of the deal on our contract because they were having issues with the sale of their home. By that time, we were committed to Briarwood, so we ran another ad to rent out one of our units and easily found tenants. We knew then that the Lord allowed those buyers to engage us in a contract so that we would go forward with the Briarwood purchase. Clearly His will for us was to purchase the property that we almost walked away from. I love when God uses drama to show us His will.

Weeks passed without a second offer on our home. It was beginning to look like maybe the Lord was going to keep us in Wall Township as there were only about five weeks left before our self-imposed deadline of Labor Day, 1998.

On a warm August evening we got an unexpected call from a lady who had attended one of our spring Open Houses but had never indicated a serious interest in our house. Explaining that her home was now under contract and due to close in October, her request was to come and see our house again. While making the appointment, I was infused with the hope that maybe we would have a contract by Labor Day after all.

Our new potential Buyer came to revisit our home with her family, and within days was asking for our attorney's name and phone number because she wanted to make an offer. The $215,000 offer was fair so we countered at just $2,000 above her number and she accepted.

Everything went smoothly and we were able to sell that property in a timely manner. The little bit of equity from that house would be the down payment and closing costs for the next purchase that the Lord had in mind for us.

THE VICTORIAN CHARMER

Chapter Five

Our Dream Property & Windfall

*A*llenhurst, New Jersey, a tiny seashore hamlet on the Atlantic Ocean, only a third of a square mile, is huge in character and appeal. Most of the homes built on the tree-lined streets, are turn-of-the-century beauties. It is a town rich in history because of the many influential people who for many years had been coming from NYC and Philadelphia to vacation on the Allenhurst beach in the summer sun.

When still living in our ranch on Francis Drive, Keith and I discovered Allenhurst while perusing a real estate magazine. We noticed older homes for sale at low price points and decided to start checking into the possibility of purchasing a home in disrepair.

Through that process, we met our trusted realtor, Gayle Billows of Gloria Nilsen & Company in Ocean Township, who has patiently worked with us on both buying and selling properties in Monmouth County, NJ. We casually studied the Allenhurst market for a few years while contemplating a move to that quaint town.

Our thought was that if we suddenly found a must-have property, we would list our Wall Township home immediately and make the sale a contract contingency. Instead, we ended up selling our house before finding a property in Allenhurst that we could afford to purchase.

It was the end of August, 1998; we had less than two months to move and we didn't have a specific house in mind. Our prayer was that we would be able to one day live in Allenhurst, but we were not sure that was God's plan for us. Though winter rentals are plentiful at the Jersey Shore in the fall, most all of them are furnished. However, it did seem prudent to consider moving twice rather than to make a quick decision on buying a home that we might later regret. To our surprise, the newspaper had a winter rental listed in Allenhurst that sounded perfect.

We called the Landlord, Tom Landes, and asked if he would consider renting to us without furnishings. He said he could store most of his belongings in his two-car garage as long as we did not need to use it ourselves. That was an amazing answer to prayer, as most landlords would not have been willing to accommodate our request.

The 1917 rental property was a grand, four-bedroom, two-and-a-half-bath, white stucco, center hall colonial home, with beautiful hardwood floors and a large maple-floored front porch. The double-hung windows were very old and pretty with prairie mullions on the upper portions. A huge fieldstone fireplace was the focal point of the living room and the spacious dining room was well-suited for entertaining. Since the house was in need of renovations, the $1200 monthly price tag seemed appropriate and affordable. At one point we asked Tom if he would consider selling the house, but he was not at all interested.

During my favorite season of the year, we sold our house in Wall Township and moved to the Corlies Avenue rental in Allenhurst. Old sycamore trees lined most of the streets, forming arches of color in hues of orange, gold and bronze. With the ocean only three blocks from our house, it felt like we were living in a storybook setting; we wondered if we would only have the pleasure of living in Allenhurst for the short term of our lease or if God would give us the desire of our hearts and make Allenhurst a more permanent place to live. It was such a joy to live in that delightful hamlet and we were grateful for whatever time we would be there, but how we longed to be able to stay.

As we continued to trust the Lord for our future, we took a break from property searches since we had just signed an eight month lease, but we never stopped praying about the next house.

The House across the Street

Four months before moving to Allenhurst, we attended a Sunday afternoon Open House on Corlies Avenue, at a house caddy-corner across the street from our future winter rental. The weather was dismal and so was the house. At that time, the asking price was $279,000 and as Keith and I walked through, we could not imagine investing in a property that needed

> **Buying Tip:**
>
> A contractor can prepare a list of renovation costs *before* making an offer so you know ahead of time what you're getting into.

so much rehabilitation. Because we knew the Allenhurst market so well, it also seemed to us that the house was over-priced. We walked away and only mentioned to Gayle in passing that we had visited. Neither one of us thought that was the house for us.

By the time we moved in across the street, the price of that old behemoth had dropped to $259,000, but it still was of no interest. By December of 1998, when it was time to begin to start looking for a permanent home, the price was lowered to $229,000. The property was part of an estate sale and the five siblings who inherited the house were very anxious to get their money, and lighten their load of responsibility.

At the low price of $229,000, this turn-of-the-century seashore Victorian suddenly became a property of strong interest to us and the subject of many more prayers. Keith spent hours on the front porch of our rental house gazing across the street at the only house in town that we could comfortably afford. The house had lots of curb appeal with a wrap-around front porch shaded with black and white stripped awnings and a two-story turret, showcasing beautiful elongated old Victorian windows. While we knew the renovations would be more costly than simple cosmetics, we decided to reconsider that property. We loved Allenhurst and really did not want to leave.

The decision was made to hire a contractor to prepare a laundry list of renovation costs *before* making an offer to be sure we knew what we were getting ourselves into. For example, there was a cracked and bulging cement wall in the basement, which likely scared away other potential buyers. Our contractor said that the wall was not a huge issue. He indicated that for $8,000 we could hire a company to replace the wall. His laundry list totaled about $40,000 not including the painting which we planned to do ourselves. One hundred dollars was a small price to pay for all that information.

Our offer of $185,000 was put together with Gayle's help. Included was our renovations list on the contractor's letterhead to show how we arrived at that price. (We left a $5,000 cushion in case the sellers countered our offer.) The morning that Gayle was to submit the contract, I was having some quiet meditation and I felt a very strong impression in my spirit to immediately put together a letter to accompany our offer. I remember the essence of what I said after the salutation:

"We are including with our offer a list of expenses that we will incur in the renovation of your home, should we have the opportunity to purchase from you. It is not our intention to insult you with the price we are offering, but we have a limited budget for the repairs, and the purchase of your property. Understanding that this is your family estate and the place where you grew up, we want you to know that, should we become the new owners, you are welcome

to stop in for coffee and a visit when you are in town. Our hope and prayer is that you will give our offer serious consideration.
Sincerely, Linda and Keith Abrams"

Offer Accepted

After faxing the cover letter off to Gayle, the paperwork was submitted to the listing realtor that morning. Our homework was complete and the response was in God's hands. Keith and I left town that afternoon for a company Christmas dinner in Manhattan. While dining with colleagues, Keith got a call on his cell phone from Gayle. The Sellers had accepted our offer without countering. We were thrilled! The decorator in me started mentally planning the details for the interior while I was praying for the house inspection that was yet to come.

One of the attractions of the 3200-square-foot house was the unique layout. The foyer boasted a turned staircase of ornate, white, cast iron balusters and French doors leading to the dining room. Showcasing the base of the turret, the dining room had been relocated to the front of the house. Under the upper portion of the staircase was the entrance to the L-shaped kitchen

> **Buying Tip:**
>
> **Do your home work and leave the outcome to God.**

and off the kitchen through one door was a huge living room. Also attached to the kitchen was small den and potential office. A cozy powder room with antique brass faucets mounted on a fluted pedestal sink under an oval mirror had been decorated to reflect the Victorian character of the house. That powder room was the only room in the house that did not need immediate attention.

Upstairs were four bedrooms and two full baths. The yellow-tiled bathroom appeared to never have been updated since the house was built in 1904, but the hot pink bathroom was clearly a 50's renovation. The prettiest room upstairs was the guest bedroom because of the architecture of the turret. It appeared however, when looking at the outside of the house, a bedroom window had been covered over when the white vinyl siding was installed. Our goal was to replace it at some point in the future.

The day of the house inspection, Keith and I joined in on the tour. The weather was cloudy, which can be a downer when 'dreary' is the feeling in almost every room. As we spent more time in the house, Keith was becoming visibly depressed over the amount of work the house needed. The kitchen needed extensive cleaning, especially the flat-faced birch cabinets that appeared to have been built on the job, sometime mid-century. The cabinetry needed to either be replaced, or get a much needed facelift. The old, linoleum-covered, uneven kitchen floor clearly was an eyesore. The heating system was so old and broken that when turned on, it made an exploding type of noise that was truly frightening. Replacing the heating system and adding central air would be a top priority. Throughout the day, I assured Keith that we could work our magic and end up with a lovely home. Thankfully, he trusted my opinion and wasn't depressed for long.

Roof Inspection

When our contractor put together the costs of renovations before we made our offer, one important element: the roof was not discussed. Our house inspector took us up in the attic to show us that the original cedar shakes were visible from the inside because no plywood had ever been laid. The asphalt shingles had been installed over top of the cedar shingles, without insulation, so it was clear that a whole new roof would be necessary. We immediately called a roofer who we knew well, to come over and give us an estimate. Given the height of the house and the need for new plywood, the estimate was $15,000, which had not been previously budgeted.

We then wrote another letter to the homeowners via their realtor, with an explanation of our dilemma. Since our original contract was subject to a house inspection, we still had the opportunity to walk away from the deal if the report was worse than anticipated. Not knowing where we could come up with the additional money, we decided to ask the homeowners for a $15,000 reduction in the selling price.

In our letter, we stated that we thought the house was worth the $185,000 that we had previously offered, even with the need for a new roof, but that we simply didn't have the extra funds. We made it clear that we would understand if they wanted to terminate our agreement and look for another buyer.

For a few days, we heard nothing back. We called Gayle to let her know that we had no response. She immediately contacted the other realtor who checked into the matter. As it turned out, the Seller's lawyer never contacted them about our second letter. As soon as the Sellers found out that we needed them to lower the asking price to $170,000, they agreed to the new price and our contract was revised downward. We closed on Corlies Avenue early in January 1999, and were able to supervise the renovations from our winter rental across the street. How convenient!

The Renovations Begin

Hiring Gene Vincenzi was one of the best decisions that we made in real estate investing. It is *not* easy to locate a *competent* contractor, and finding Gene was another blessing from the Lord.

Late one afternoon, while we were still living in Wall Township, I was leaving the Post Office and stopped behind a van with signage that read, *Specializing in Old Home Restorations*. He turned left and I made a right out of the parking lot.

As soon as we went our separate ways, I got a very strong sense in my spirit that I needed to turn around and follow that van to get the phone number for future reference. We still did not have a contract on Francis Drive in Wall, but since we had been looking at old homes in Allenhurst, I thought we might need whoever was behind the wheel of that van to help us someday.

Immediately I turned around and went speeding down the road to find that van. Fortunately it was stopped at a red light and I was able to scribble the phone number down on a scrap of paper. I tucked that name and number away in a safe place, and when the time came for us to hire a contractor to look at Corlies Avenue with us, Eugene G Vincenzi, owner of Home Restoration & Remodeling in Wall, NJ is the man we called.

After checking a few of Gene's references, we hired him to handle much of the project for us. Gene was kind enough to refer us to a good electrician, among others. Overall, our project was *not* a nightmare because of God and Gene.

One of the ideas that Gene suggested was to remove the French doors between the dining room and foyer, and tear out the upper portion of the walls on either side of the doorway. He would leave a half-wall on each side and install columns from the top of the half walls to the ceiling. It was an innovative concept because, opening up those walls made both the dining room and the foyer feel so much larger. Keith and I agreed that the small extra cost was well worth it.

Our large kitchen would only get a facelift until we could afford to tear out the old cabinets and start over. Even the beige Formica countertops would have to wait. Since I always wanted a white kitchen, the logical solution was to paint the cabinets white. That, I knew, would be a huge project. An extended out-of-town business trip for Keith gave me two weeks to tackle and almost complete the job. All the grimy cabinets had to be scraped and cleaned thoroughly with TSP, a cleaning product, available at paint and hardware stores. Prepping the wood alone took several days, even after all the doors had been removed.

Good work space was created by setting up saw horses in the kitchen, topped with a couple of old doors. On those make-shift tables, I laid out all the cabinet doors and drawers. After the thorough cleaning, I primed everything with an oil-based paint (only necessary for the first coat) and followed up with two coats of latex semi-gloss white. Because the doors were so plain, I decided to give them a Victorian flair by gluing thin wood appliqués of bundled wheat, in the center of each door. The appliqués got two coats of paint, one primer and one latex coat before being applied with wood glue. New brushed nickel hardware added luster to our 'renewed' white kitchen.

The walls in the dining area of the room were painted a soft yellow and in the working areas, we chose a deep Caribbean blue. We had a few other needs so I kept an eye on the classifieds in the newspaper. (Now I use *Craig's List* for both buying and selling, with great success.) An ad appeared for a quality stainless steel sink and faucet for $25. Included in the ad, was a Dekor gas cook top for $75 (usually valued at $1,000 brand new). I immediately made an appointment to drive out to the lady's house with cash, confident that I would make the purchase of both.

While looking at the sink and cooktop, I noticed a beautiful, oval, tiger oak, hand-carved pedestal table with five Victorian chairs in a walnut stain. The lady was asking $300 for the set. The table looked like an antique, but the chairs were not. We ended up buying the table and chairs, a perfect addition to our updated space. What I would later find out from a furniture restoration company is that my table was a true antique, worth about $2300, obviously a super investment.

A creamy, stone-like ceramic tile floor was installed in the kitchen after we lived on a new plywood floor for months, trying to decide what type of surface we wanted. There are pros and cons to various floors. Ceramic has a reputation for being unforgiving if you drop breakable items, hard on feet and legs, but so beautiful when installed. An upscale vinyl tile is more practical, but often there is no difference in price. Keith decided that he didn't want to pay the same money for a 'knock off' as for real ceramic. We did not regret our decision.

Hardwood floors in the living and dining rooms were professionally refinished. We tackled the hardwoods in the bedrooms ourselves to save money. For the foyer, we chose a bright, floral print, Victorian-style carpet which created a wow factor against the white staircase. Painting was our job and all the rooms were in need of better color choices.

During the first stage of renovating, it was clear that we would not immediately have enough money to do everything to the house that we envisioned. It was important to tackle everything on Gene's list, but some projects, like the yellow bathroom would have to wait until we could catch our breath and save some more money. Older homes are often an endless project, and we did not want the rehabilitation of our home to consume us. It was time to take a 'reno' break and enjoy our new home with grateful hearts for what had been accomplished.

A Challenging Change

Six months after we moved from our winter rental into what became our first 'dream house,' Keith came home from work and told me that he was losing his job with the company he had been serving for almost 15 years. Over time, Keith's diligent service took him from middle management to a much higher paying position as a senior corporate manager in a multi-million dollar organization. With every promotion, Keith excelled and was propelled to a level he could not have imagined for himself. Thankfully, those at the top awarded Keith with a generous severance package, paying him his full salary for the next nine months, allowing him ample time to find another job.

Surely the Sovereign Lord does nothing without
revealing His plan to His servants
Amos 3:7

The news could have been overwhelming, but both Keith and I were confident that the Lord had another door He would open for us. We knew that our responsibility as believers is to walk closely with Him so that we can sense His direction whenever it comes.

The fact that Keith had such a wonderful severance plan in place made trusting the Lord for answers much easier. As I write this book I know that millions of Americans have lost jobs without such a cushion; for those people, trusting the Lord takes on a whole new dimension. I have great admiration for those who are empowered to trust God without any knowledge of how they will pay the bills as they come in.

> Our responsibility as believers is to walk closely with God so that we can sense His direction whenever it comes.

To be sure, a high paying executive position is not easily replaced. Keith began his search, which was almost a full-time job, and continued to seek employment for many months without success. We prayed diligently during that time, but even interviews were almost non-existent.

Finally, after being encouraged by a friend, Keith decided to market long-term care insurance. Initially, we thought the opportunity offered the best of both worlds, an affiliation with a large well-known corporation, and status as an independent consultant.

The problem turned out to be that most of Keith's day was spent on the phone trying to make appointments with people who really didn't want to sit down and discuss 'end-of-life realities.' For every 40 or more calls, Keith might get one appointment, which was just step one in the sales process. During the six months that he worked in that industry, Keith only made a few sales and then the unthinkable happened.

Early in the day on 9/11, Keith promptly started his phone work, totally unaware of what was happening not far from our home. The first man he called was surprised to hear from a salesman in light of the horrific news on television. Realizing that Keith had not heard the news, he politely suggested we turn on the TV.

Like most of America, we spent the day watching that horrific event in disbelief; mindful that it would forever change our Country. Within hours we received word that friends of ours, Don and Jean Peterson perished on the flight that went down in Pennsylvania. We believe Don was one of the heroes who fought the terrorists, as he was a true patriot willing to die for his beloved Country.

Soon we were informed that one of our campaign workers (we had been working on the NJ Governor's campaign all during 2001) lost his dad in one of the Twin Towers. Wanting to represent the campaign, we would attend Al's funeral as well. Because all three of those dear souls loved the Lord when they died, their funerals were a tribute to lives well-lived, and hopeful celebrations of the Heaven where they would spend eternity.

Changing Course

After 9/11 it seemed that people were wondering if they would ever live long enough to need long-term care, making the sales of such policies even more challenging. Keith was not enjoying this new career. We agreed that it was time to look for an existing business to purchase; one that was producing good cash flow. A start-up business was not a consideration at that time. Keith gave up his independent contractor status as a Long Term Care Consultant and began a full-time search for an existing company in the commercial market. He was open to many different industries, so his search was broad and eventually included other nearby states.

> **Buying Tip:**
>
> A buyer should only trust what a seller can prove.

It would be another nine months before we closed on an automotive service center and parts store in Townsend, Delaware. Initially, we looked within a 60-mile radius of our home, hoping that we could stay in Allenhurst. However, we did not find anything worth the asking price, or with good records to prove the numbers claimed. Keith is a very wise businessman. He knows a worthy deal when he sees one and he will walk away in a heartbeat if anything seems amiss. It is amazing to us just how many business people keep poor records, and then simply want you to trust them when trying to sell their companies. A buyer should only trust what a seller can prove.

Worth the Wait

Waiting on the Lord is often challenging for His impatient children. From the day we found out that Keith would need a different path of income, until the Lord showed us His will, we had a confidence that He had a plan. However, had we known that first day that it would be three long years before Plan B would become our reality I think it might have shaken our faith to the core. It is so good that we don't know the future, and we only have to trust one day at a time.

During that long waiting period, Keith and I prayed together and devoured the classic devotional book, *Streams in the Desert*, by Mrs. Charles E. Cowman, hanging on to every promise of God that encouraged us on our journey. While the income from our duplex on Briarwood (see Chapter Seven) supplemented our living expenses in Allenhurst, there was only one month we wondered if we would be short on our mortgage payment.

In that month, when we were short more than half of the mortgage payment, we did what we always do: we simply asked God to supply our need to pay the mortgage. And He did. In the mail we received an unexpected $300 check from one of my brothers, with a note saying that he felt badly for our circumstances and hoped the enclosed 'love gift' would help. While it seemed like a small gift to him, it was huge for us and there was more on the way.

That same week, my dear friend Cynthia May flew to New Jersey to move her dad, Victor, to live with her in California. Keith and I had helped Victor on Cynthia's behalf and in her absence. Before they left town, Cynthia enclosed $500 in cash, in a lovely *Thank You* card with a note of deep gratitude. Those two gifts combined gave us the $800, the exact amount that we were short for our mortgage payment. What a joy to see the hand of God so dramatically meet our needs that month.

Nationally, the real estate market was in a strong upward turn during the time that we were looking to buy a business. However, something else was happening in Allenhurst, making it a unique selling market. Wealthy business people from Brooklyn, NY, were coming to Allenhurst looking to buy summer homes near the beach. Allenhurst's proximity to New York City was driving up the cost of homes at a far more rapid pace than most other towns at the Shore. As word got out about how much money homes were selling for in 2001, the rapid rise in equity seemed surreal.

In 2002, after a 9 month search, we found a company to purchase that was a perfect fit for Keith. Early in his career he had worked for an automobile conglomerate as a parts manager in middle management for several car dealerships, working closely with service managers. That experience, along with his

> It is so important that in all areas of life we are totally truthful about our intentions, because God will not honor deceit.

work at the corporate management level in information technology, provided Keith with vast knowledge of the auto industry. A service center and parts store with significant cash flow, along with good records, was the answer to our prayers. Finding just the right business was certainly worth the time we had to wait.

Our Unexpected Windfall

The decision was made to purchase what would become *Townsend Motor World, T/A Auto Doctors* in Delaware. Selling our Allenhurst house was now not optional, it was crucial. In order to be able to relocate and buy a company, we would need the equity that had been building in our Victorian home. Earlier in the year, we listed it with Gayle, but our house didn't sell. In order to be able to put a deposit down on the business, we needed to refinance our home, but typically, that cannot be done while the house is on the market. Most banks will not want to refinance a property short-term, as they make most of their money on long-term agreements.

Concerned that it would be difficult to find a bank to refinance a house that we would clearly need to sell, we asked the Lord to open doors for us and honestly explained our circumstances to several bankers. We told them that we needed to refinance our house for immediate cash, but that once we got the money, we would have to try to sell the house in order to relocate. Another challenge was that Keith was still without income. It is so important that in all areas of life we are totally truthful about our intentions, because God will not honor deceit.

> **Buying Tip:**
>
> **The importance of maintaining good credit cannot be overstated.**

The Lord did open a door for us at a local bank. The banker knew exactly what we were about to do, but because of our excellent credit scores and our ability to present the paperwork on what Keith's salary would be once he owned the company, we were able to refinance in a few days. Getting approval on the refinance of our Allenhurst home was totally a 'God thing.' The importance of maintaining good credit cannot be overstated. We have tried to instill in our children the value of superior credit scores. As a couple, we have always been diligent about paying our bills on time, and that has been a tremendous help in our success as investors.

In an effort to be able to keep the bulk of our equity so that we would have enough money for a new business and our personal residence, we decided to try to sell Allenhurst ourselves, but were willing to work with realtors who might have interested buyers. Shortly after we received our large refi check, a For Sale by Owner sign went up on our front lawn. Our asking price was $609,000. After the company we were

> **Selling Fact:**
>
> **Often the sale of older homes takes longer than newer and new homes.**

buying in Delaware had been thoroughly vetted, the closing date for our new business was set for a day in August, 2002. Thankfully, we were able to get enough money from the refinance bank to not only buy the business, but to also purchase a townhouse in Wilmington. Our plan was to stay in the townhouse until the sale of our big house in Allenhurst was complete. At that point we would have the money to buy a traditional home.

We soon discovered that the sale of older homes takes longer than newer and new homes. Most people do not want the challenges that come from owning an older property. Repairs are generally more costly and, unless a home has been totally renovated, there are endless projects. That being said, from our perspective, generally there is an undeniable charm in older homes that is difficult to duplicate.

Living in our Allenhurst house felt as if we had stepped back in time. I couldn't imagine why anyone would not want to buy our home, but realistically, I knew the house needed more work. The Lord would need to send a buyer who had vision for the rooms that we had only painted.

While we were waiting for a buyer, our friend Annie moved into the Allenhurst house so that it would not be vacant while we were living in Delaware. She was also able to show the house since we were still trying to market it on our own and were always out of town. Annie was a real blessing to us.

As we had expected, most of the people who wanted to see the house were from New York. Some came with a realtor, while others acted as their own agents.

One day a real estate agent came with a young couple from Brooklyn. They really liked our home and made an offer. After some negotiating we agreed to a sales price of $585,000.

The equity we accumulated was a modern day miracle. Considering that we only paid $170,000 for the Corlies Avenue house and invested $60,000 in renovations, we ended up with a

$355,000 windfall! That is how much the house had appreciated during those three-plus years! What was really exciting was that for each year we waited on the Lord for answers, wondering why He was being so slow, the value of our home rose so fast that it matched Keith's former annual corporate salary. Clearly time was on our side, not against us. But it was only in looking back that we could see the hand of God.

> God truly knows what He is doing, and He absolutely is a God who can be trusted.

In the midst of waiting on the Lord, our faith was often challenged, but we did persevere, believing God would reveal His plan. He truly knows what He is doing, and He absolutely *is* a God who can be trusted. Not many houses across America appreciate over $100,000 per year. God knows the end from the beginning and yet we struggle to trust Him.

Trust in the Lord with all your heart and lean not on your own understanding; in all your ways acknowledge Him, and He will make your paths straight.
Proverbs 3:5

Life in Allenhurst was wonderful while it lasted. An invitation had been extended to me to join the local garden club, which Keith thought was funny because I don't like to get my hands dirty. I figured I would just have to keep garden gloves handy. Thankfully, it turned out to be more of a social group, but we did work together to beautify Main Street by planting seasonal flowers in huge cement containers.

Keith and I were members of the *Allenhurst Homeowners Association* which also added activities to our social agenda. During the Christmas season, it was interesting to attend meetings and parties in the other older homes in town and see how they were designed and decorated. Our local friends and neighbors were gracious to us. We felt very welcomed in Allenhurst, even from the early days of our winter rental, and knew we would miss the small town experience once we arrived in the City of Wilmington. When all the plans had been worked out, we were sure that the Lord was closing the Allenhurst chapter of our lives and we tried not to be sad.

THE VILLA

Chapter Six

Villa Property with a View

*B*ut I *was* sad. Heading west from Allenhurst to Wilmington, alone in my packed car with the evening sun directly ahead, I began to cry. Moving from New Jersey, a state that I had always loved and from idyllic Allenhurst, really challenged me, even though I thought I was prepared. Helen Keller once said, "Life is a daring adventure, or nothing." My prayer was that I would see my new life in Delaware as an adventure. I thanked the Lord for Keith's new career opportunity and felt gratitude that returning to Jersey for visits was a simple trip over a bridge. My parents were still in their homestead, only a two-hour drive from our new home. By the time I arrived at our townhouse, I was hopeful and grateful.

Buying Online

The acquisition of our amazing 20-year-old townhouse was unique. Once Keith had a contract to buy his business, we used our old standby, *Realtor.com*, to search the listings in Wilmington.

A house of interest came up, and since the realtor in the photo, looked like a nice lady (not the ideal way to choose a realtor), we called Linda LaPense to request a copy of the listing of an old sea captain's home. Impressed with the details, we made an appointment to see the property with Linda. Upon careful analysis of the 100-year-old place, we determined we were not ready for another major, old home renovation project. The tour was fun and ended with Linda wanting us to meet her husband, Christian, with whom she partnered in marketing properties.

Awhile later we returned to Wilmington and toured more properties, this time with Christian LaPense. Not having found anything of particular interest, we ended the day at the real estate office chatting with the LaPense's. As we were about to leave, Christian mentioned that he was on his way to list a townhouse that might be worth checking out. When he told us the listing price would be about $189,000, we politely told him that we didn't want to pay that much for a townhouse that was likely to be a temporary home for us.

A week later, Keith was perusing the *Realtor.com* website when he came across a fantastic townhouse with panoramic views of the Delaware River from multiple levels. The extensive photos showcased a four-level end unit with: two fieldstone fireplaces, hardwood floors, cherry doors, crown moldings and a screened-in porch overlooking a lush backyard. It looked fabulous.

When we saw that the contact realtor was Christian LaPense, and the listing price was $189,000, we were sure that was the townhouse Christian mentioned to us the week before. The listing notes indicated that the house was undergoing some renovations and would not be able to be shown until after Memorial Day, a few weeks later.

Keith called Christian immediately and made a full-price offer of $189,000, 'sight unseen,' subject to our initial inspection. We also asked that all work on the property cease, since we prefer to buy "As-Is" and do our own decorating. The seller agreed and within 24 hours we had a contract.

Normally, we do not recommend making a purchase decision without at least one tour. However, since the contract was written, "subject to the inspection of Buyer," we knew that if we didn't like it when we saw it, the contract could and would be voided. It was important to have a written document so that we didn't find ourselves in a bidding war. This townhouse seemed so wonderful, our concern was that many others would be interested and we were hoping that God wanted us to have it.

Though "a picture is worth a thousand words," often there is no substitute for the real experience. Our visit to the property, which we fondly refer to as 'The Villa' because the address was Seton Villa Lane, did not disappoint. The Villa was more than we could have hoped for. The online photos did not do it justice.

The ground floor consisted of a one-car garage, a laundry room, and a large family room with an eight-foot sliding glass door leading out to a cement patio. The centerpiece of the backyard was a large magnolia tree, surrounded by sea grass bushes, a Japanese maple tree, rosebushes, hydrangeas and more. Though it needed to be tamed, the landscaping was luscious.

The front door led us into a foyer with steps going down on the right into the family room, and steps going up on the left to the second level of the main living area. At the top of the steps, to the left was the kitchen; straight ahead was the dining room, which opened to a large living room. A wood-burning fireplace centered on the wall was flanked by six-foot sliding doors that led out to a 10x20 foot screened porch. Wonderful views of the Delaware River, which was only about a half mile away, were a huge selling feature. A powder room with a mahogany vanity and marble top completed the second level, but the best was still to come.

As we made our way to the third level, with the guest room and the master bedroom, we were feeling very confident that we would want to go through with the sale. Straight ahead from the top step, looking toward the back of the house, a massive fieldstone fireplace beckoned us to the master bedroom. As we entered, we stood in complete amazement, not knowing where to look first. The massive 13x20 foot room had a vaulted ceiling with skylights. As in the living room below, two six-foot sliding glass doors on either side of the fireplace lead out to a balcony with panoramic views of the Delaware River. We were having a "WOW" experience, as we could see for miles, up and down the river, and across to New Jersey. We knew we found the place we were looking for.

The fourth level was a loft overlooking the master suite, accessed by a spiral stair case. The loft became Keith's office, where the only way to get his large desk into the space was to remove several portions of the railings that were bolted into the floor and hoist the desk up from our bedroom below. Due to some necessary repairs that could not be seen online, we renegotiated the sale price down to $182,000.

The Villa got a facelift that was mostly cosmetic, but we also added a new roof and replaced some windows and siding, sprucing things up in a short period of time. We felt so blessed in our new home. It was really neat to watch the freighters run up and down the river. On Saturdays we often saw cruise ships going to and from the port in Philadelphia.

The Lord moved us out of one delightful home into another, and I was no longer sad. Our Allenhurst house sold in February of 2003, eight months after we moved into the Villa, bringing closure to the long New Jersey chapter of our lives.

Our Aging Parents

By June of that year my parent's health was deteriorating. Dad had been diagnosed with a slow growing cancer, and Mom's stroke several years earlier resulted in vascular dementia which was not improving. Keith and I convinced my family that it would be best for my parents to leave River Vale and come to live with us in Delaware. Since the townhouse was not big enough for all four of us, we opted to rent it out, and together with my parents, we bought an economical home that would adequately accommodate all of us. Keith and I would pay the mortgage once our townhouse was rented.

It was important for us to find something quickly, but there was not a lot of inventory from which to choose. The house that turned out to be perfect, a four-level split, was only a few miles away on Butler Avenue. My parents used the two lower levels, and Keith and I managed the main living areas of the upper two floors. Often we would bring Mom and Dad up to sit with us in our living room so that they would not feel isolated. They ate all their meals with us as well.

My siblings came to Jersey to dismantle my parent's home and bring some of the furniture to Delaware. We moved all of our personal furniture out of the Villa over to Butler Avenue, so appropriately named, as there we would care for Mom and Dad with the help of a full-time home health aide. A few months after we moved to Butler, we found tenants for the townhouse. By the end of October, we were all settled in.

Originally, it was Keith's idea to bring Mom and Dad to live with us. He has a strong Biblical view on the importance of children caring for aging parents. Keith is an intense proponent of family being responsible for family. I am forever grateful for his devotion to my parents and his participation in helping me to look after them. What a gift to be able to honor my parents at Butler for a total of ten months.

If a widow has children or grandchildren,
these should learn first of all to put their religion into practice
by caring for their own family and so repaying their parents
and grandparents, for this is pleasing to God.
1 Timothy 5: 4

Caring for aging parents is challenging and a huge commitment. Though I have quoted the above verse to encourage, my purpose is not to lay a guilt trip on any of my readers. Circumstances are different in every family, and some simply don't have the resources whether emotional or financial, to take care of aging relatives. It is our responsibility to go to God and seek His will for our lives and the future of our loved ones. *If* He is calling us to become more involved in caring for those we love, the Lord will give us the answers we seek, the grace to respond and rewards above and beyond our call of duty.

> Caring for aging parents is challenging and a huge commitment. Circumstances are different in every family, and some simply don't have the resources whether emotional or financial, to take care of aging relatives.

Looking after two parents with various stages of dementia was not without comic relief. When Dad needed a hospital bed, we placed it right next to my parent's double bed without any space in between. Mom and Dad always had a wonderful marriage. They adored one another, and were very affectionate throughout their lives. Dad didn't want to sleep in a hospital bed unless he could be very near to Mom. We did, however, keep the guard rails up to try to keep Dad in his bed.

Our bedroom was directly above theirs, which proved to be very helpful. Because of the cancer, Dad had a chronic cough, but due to their dementia, neither parent had enough cognitive thought to get Dad a cough drop. When I would hear him coughing during the night, I would get up and go down stairs to offer Dad a lozenge.

One night I woke up in the middle of the night and heard Dad and Mom giggling together. I went down to check up on them, wondering what all the laughter was about. Much to my surprise, when I came into the bedroom, I saw that Mom had climbed over the guard rail, into the hospital bed with Dad. When I asked what they were doing, they said, almost

> It is so gratifying to be able to honor our parents later on in life by caring for them.

in unison, that they wanted to be closer to each other. They were a hoot, and I got a good laugh. Assuring them that there wasn't room for both of them in that small bed, I was able to coax Mom back into her bed, with the hope that they would fall asleep, so that I could get some rest as well.

For those currently caring for loved ones, or considering the sacrifice of becoming a caretaker, be encouraged. Get as much help as possible, but seize the opportunity. It is so gratifying to be able to honor our parents later on in life by caring for them. Honestly, it is a lot of work, but the rewards far outweigh the challenges. Keith and I look back on those months spent with Mom and Dad, with gratitude for the opportunity and the grace to bless them. It is part of the legacy that we leave for our children.

As stated previously, Dad passed away on June 18, 2004. We were able to keep him home with us by adding round-the-clock nursing care during his last week of life. The Lord gave me the joy of being at his bedside the moment that he passed from this life to the next. As soon as Dad took his last breath, a smile came over his face and I knew in that instant he was in Heaven! What a gift God gave me that day. I am forever grateful.

Mom's New Home

Shortly after Dad's passing, Mom was like a lost puppy. While he was alive, she would sit and hold his hand, which I am sure gave her a sense of purpose. Now that Dad was gone, Mom was bored and not easily entertained. Keith and I had no other family near us, so there were few visitors to spend any time with Mom. It soon became clear that keeping my mother with us was not in her best interest. Because of her dementia, Mom needed far more stimulation than we could provide. Television all day long was not an option.

We began thinking about an alternative plan. Years earlier, Mom talked about the possibility of retiring in St. Louis where three of her children and their families lived, but Dad never really wanted to leave New Jersey. Our new thought was that if we could find a reputable assisted living residence in the St Louis area, Mom could have lots of family visitors while being able to participate in programs designed for those with similar challenges. A *Sunrise Assisted Living* was opening a new facility within a ten-minute radius of my sister and two brothers. It was the perfect solution.

> There truly are some circumstances when assisted living facilities can be a better alternative to family care.

The last weekend in July, I flew with Mom to St. Louis to get her moved in with the help of our family members. She had a cheerful, bright, private room with a shared bath. The residents ate chef-prepared food in a restaurant-style dining room with linen napkins and table cloths, amid antique reproductions in the ambiance of an old mansion. The décor of the common areas was so beautiful and luxurious, the whole facility felt like a home with a staff of friendly and helpful caretakers who seemed to love the residents.

As my plane left the runway, I shed a few tears, but I knew that my very social mother would be much happier at *Sunrise* than she would have been had we kept her in Wilmington. There truly are some circumstances when assisted living facilities can be a better alternative to family care. As a family we prayed extensively before making the decision to place Mom at *Sunrise*. On the way home, I had a peace about our decision, and could not have known that *Sunrise* would be Mom's 'home' for the next five years.

Our Return to The Villa

Due to capital gains tax law, Keith and I had to stay in the Butler house for one more year so that we would not have to pay taxes when we sold the property. After our tenants moved out of the townhouse, we decided to renovate the kitchen and bathrooms while the house was empty. When the time came, we listed the Butler Avenue house with Christian LaPense and prayed for a sale.

The Lord sent us a buyer within a few months. However, our deal fell apart when the home inspector found an issue with one of our foundation walls. The finished basement had been paneled and it was difficult to see that the wall was bowed. When one stood sideways against the wall, the bowing was obvious. Unfortunately, our initial home inspector missed it, and now it would have to be fixed, so that we could sell the house. It was a $9,000 expense that we wished we had not incurred, but there were no other options. Shortly after the repairs were complete, the Lord sent us a new buyer. After a seamless sale, in October we were back at the Villa.

With the kitchen and bath renovations complete, our Villa was more delightful than ever. My brother Gary owns a very success-ful high-end cabinet design company, The *G. Lutjens Company* in Paterson, New Jersey. Gary was kind enough to sell us cherry-stained birch cabinets at an affordable price. Some of our remodel decisions were based on the idea that we wanted to stay put for awhile.

One of the important changes was transitioning the family room into a bedroom by adding a door. The room already had a closet and though I was using the space for my office, turning a two-bedroom unit into a three-bedroom added property value. We felt sure that we would be there for at least five years. By that time in my adult life, I had moved 16 times and I really didn't want to relocate anytime soon. We could not have known that the Lord's plans were vastly different. In time, they would be revealed.

THE DUPLEX

Chapter Seven

Investment Properties

Sicklerville, New Jersey

E arly in our marriage, Keith and I discussed real estate investing. We felt that our combined talents, Keith's in business and finance and mine in interior decorating could serve us well in purchasing homes in disrepair to either resell or rent. It seemed prudent for us to begin with a modestly-priced single family dwelling. Unfortunately, because we lived in one of the most expensive counties in the United States, we needed to roam beyond our immediate area in search of a deal we could afford. In Sicklerville,

> **Buying Tip:**
>
> **Once a certain period of time has passed, if a property has not been sold to an owner-occupied buyer, HUD will make the property available to investors.**

New Jersey, about one and a half hours from our home in Wall Township, we found a HUD (Housing & Urban Development) foreclosure on the market for $34,000. It is important to note that often HUD properties may only be purchased by owner-occupant buyers. However, once a certain period of time has passed, if a property has not been sold to an owner-occupied buyer, HUD will make the property available to investors. This particular property had, in fact, become available to investors and needed mostly cosmetic repairs. Our ability to handle the project would keep our potential rehab expenses to a minimum.

The foreclosure agent, Tony, told us that the government would not negotiate the $34,000 price on a HUD property, especially this one because the price had already been reduced. We decided to ignore that advice and make a lower offer of $30,000, believing that we really didn't have anything to lose. There was certainly no fear of offending the federal government. To our surprise, HUD accepted our offer. Sometimes when the Lord allows unusual circumstances, it is His way to confirm His will. Normally, we look for more than one confirmation to help us discern the will of God.

After praying about the purchase and feeling led to proceed, we borrowed the $30,000 from my parents, paid cash for the townhouse and because we didn't have much of a savings account, we used our credit cards to finance the repairs. In lieu of a typical vacation that summer, Keith chose to add vacation days to Saturdays, allowing for multiple three-day weekends. Much of July and August was spent 'schlepping' ourselves back and forth to Camden County with our tools and our vision.

By day we worked long hours, sometimes returning home the same evening and other times by night, forcing us to sleep without comfort on a crude air mattress in the townhouse. Initially we cleaned the property as thoroughly as possible so that 'camping out' would be bearable.

After purchasing a new heat pump with a professional installation, the first task on our list was to rip out the urine-drenched

> **Buying Tip:**
>
> Occasionally, foreclosures are purchased with the help of realtors who specialize in distress sales. When it is time to sell after finishing a rehab project, traditional realtors are the best choice to help find qualified buyers.

carpeting on the first floor in the living room and dining room. The carpet and padding had to be cut and tied in manageable pieces. In many municipalities, small bundling is a requirement for pickup. The house was built on a slab, and since concrete is porous, the carpet removal was only step one in ridding the floor of the pet urine smell.

We poured an oil-based orange citrus cleaning product full strength all over the cement. For weeks while we were working on other projects, we ran an expensive Alpine Air Purifier (valued in the $500 range) to finish the job. Within a few weeks the pet smell was completely gone. We were then able to have the new carpeting installed, which really made the whole house feel so much cleaner, and even newer.

Once all the painting and other projects were complete, we were ready to hire a realtor to help us sell our first investment property. Since our personal residence was at a distance, it made sense for us to solicit help with the sale. We interviewed Kathy, a realtor in Sicklerville, who had previously shown us a non-foreclosure property and who also gave us a market analysis on the townhouse. Occasionally, foreclosures are purchased with the help of realtors who specialize in distress sales. When it is time to sell after finishing a rehab project, a traditional realtor is the best choice to help find qualified buyers.

> **Buying Tip:**
>
> Even if a housing complex looks appealing, it is wise to contact the local police department before making a purchase, to inquire about the neighborhood.

What we did not know when we purchased this property was that, though the exterior was not run down and most of the surrounding properties appeared to be well-maintained; this particular complex was *not* in an up-and-coming area. We soon realized that the price is usually the first clue. All summer we prayed for our potential buyer, but the more time we learned about that area, the more we became concerned about how long we might have to wait for a sale.

Even if a housing complex looks appealing, it is wise to contact the local police department before making a purchase to inquire about the neighborhood. It is important to check on whether they get abnormal levels of domestic violence calls, break-ins, and/or whether multiple drug deals are an issue. Generally, police departments are very helpful in answering these questions.

While the neighborhood we chose was relatively safe and stable, as we became more acquainted with people in the area, we were beginning to hear rumors. Our property was near a development of town houses (built by the same company), that had a reputation for drug deals. Homes were not selling quickly in either section, so we knew that we would need to pray diligently for a buyer.

What amazed us is that when Kathy came over to give us a market analysis, she told us that she might have a buyer for us. We prayed about it and ultimately decided that listing with a realtor who *might* have a buyer was a better gamble than choosing a realtor with no potential buyer at all. The decision was made to list with Kathy.

Kathy explained her client's situation: The previous year Kathy met a single mom with one child, a good job and poor credit due to a student loan default. Kathy had encouraged her client to be diligent about repaying her loans, so that over time, her credit scores would improve. The client was told that if she would make any and all loan payments in a timely manner over a 12-month period of time she could be eligible for a mortgage. Kathy told us that her client had about three months to go and asked us if we would consider renting to this young mom until she could qualify for a mortgage.

> **Investing Tip:**
>
> A key component to success in real estate investing is *patience*.
>
> When seeking a viable investment property, a buyer should not be in a hurry, or feel impulsive about making a purchase.

Again we prayed for wisdom and felt led to take the chance using a 'Lease with a Contract to Buy' agreement. Not only did we want to help a single mom, but we knew it would benefit us as well. It is never good to have a property sit vacant for a long time, especially if the homeowner does not live nearby to keep a close watch.

The first time that Kathy brought her client to see our completed renovation, the townhouse was a big hit, and the young mother wanted to sign the agreement Kathy had prepared. The papers were signed for a three-month lease with the Contract-to-Buy in December, pending the mortgage commitment.

Everything went smoothly and we were able to close the sale on-time. Sometimes, I wonder what the chances were of us finding a buyer that quickly in a somewhat depressed market. Kathy was not a randomly chosen realtor. She was God's choice for that transaction.

After all our rehab expenses were paid, including the real estate commission, and my parents were paid back with interest, we made $9,000 on a $45,000 investment in six months. Some might argue that $9,000 is not a lot of money and therefore not worth the work. We would respectfully disagree. At that time in our lives it was a significant sum and we were able to use 90% of it for our portion of Sean's college tuition that year. It was also an important learning experience that would serve us well when purchasing our next investment property. It is not often that we get to earn while we learn and make such a great Return on Investment (ROI).

> **Rental Tip:**
>
> It is never good to have a property sit vacant for a long time, especially if the homeowner does not live nearby to keep a close watch.

Little did we know then how our Sicklerville opportunity would enable us to lay a foundation for large profits in the years ahead. By God's grace, that property worked out well for us.

Belmar, NJ

Once we experienced success with our Sicklerville project, we knew it would not be long before we would search for another investment property. It is important to note that a key component to success in real estate investing is *patience*. When seeking a viable investment property, a buyer should not be in a hurry, or feel impulsive about making a purchase. Buyers need to diligently seek the best property available.

After selling the townhouse in Sicklerville, while continuing to maintain our Wall Township residence, we actively searched for our second investment property for over a year before we found an amazing duplex in the seaside resort town of Belmar, New Jersey.

One Sunday afternoon late in the spring of 1998, Keith was running an errand when he spotted an Open House sign that drew him in. He was so impressed with the property that he immediately drove home to pick me up so that I, too, could take the house tour.

We were both very excited at finding such a jewel and immediately called our friendly realtor and neighbor, Joan Jacobs of Gloria Nilsen & Company, Spring Lake, to bring us a contract so we could make an offer. At that Open House, Keith and I both knew we had found the income property for which we had been praying.

Since Belmar is an older resort town, many of the two-family homes we had been touring were in disrepair, requiring lots of work and money. Some were tempting because of their charm, but we knew enough to walk away from multiple hefty projects. The duplex on Briarwood Road, however, was very different. It was quite new, only 10-years-old, and in pristine condition.

Briarwood, as we always referred to it, had been designed by a Portuguese man who believed in using quality products to build his properties. This three-level duplex had two identical 1600 square-foot apartments, one over the top of the other, stacked above a two car garage and a massive walk-out basement.

Curb appeal was all over this property as both front and back yards had been professionally landscaped. Half of the cedar-fenced back yard was grass and the balance was a massive custom deck. My initial look at the outside and walk-through the ground level made me feel certain that I would be wowed by the units above.

Each apartment could be reached by stairwells in the front and rear of the building, with windows on each landing. The apartment tours were extremely impressive. Each unit was clean and bright, a mirror image of the following:

❖ Living room/dining room combo with hardwood floors running the full width of the front of the house
❖ Huge eat-in kitchen with cherry wood finished cabinets and ceramic tiled floors
❖ Master bedroom and full bath with hardwood floors
❖ Two guest bedrooms with hardwood floors
❖ A huge guest bathroom with ceramic a tile floor

All utility lines had been divided evenly between the two apartments during the construction phase, which meant that the tenants would be responsible for all utilities including water and sewer bills. As landlords, only having to be responsible for property taxes made this a very desirable investment. This was definitely a property worth owning.

The original asking price had been $229,000. If I recall correctly, after several months, the price had been dropped to $223,900 when we took our tour. Our sale price ended up at $219,000. Cashing in a portion of Keith's pension was the source of the necessary 20% down-payment. At the time of purchase, we were able

> **Rental Tip:**
>
> It is very important for any investor in rental properties to establish a relationship with a national background check agency to which one pays a nominal fee.

to charge $1100 per unit which afforded us a profit every month from the beginning. By the time we sold the building five years later, we were getting $1800 per apartment. Briarwood was definitely a winner!

Finding tenants for Briarwood was always easy. Belmar was a popular resort town with a great rental market. However, many rental properties, while pricey, were often not well-maintained by landlords. Pristine units such as ours were a rare commodity. Often, we only had to place one ad in the newspaper, because we could get as many as 20 calls within a few days. Usually, if the prospects were truly qualified, the first people to tour the apartment paid the application fee for the credit check in order to be first for consideration of an annual rental contract.

> It is very important for any investor in rental properties to establish a relationship with a national background check agency to which one pays a nominal fee. We continue to use *AMS Ties, Inc.* in Beachwood, NJ, which is an excellent resource with a friendly and helpful staff. Unless a landlord has good information about the credit, criminal and payment history of an applicant, they cannot make an intelligent decision on tenants.

In the past, we were able to be very choosey. If an applicant had bad credit, we did not seriously consider their request. In these current economic times, we are less stringent regarding credit and pay more attention to payment history and recommendations from previous landlords. In some states where the price of homes is modest,

> **Rental Tip:**
>
> Provide a monthly cleaning service to your tenants. They love it and you are not left with a filthy mess when they vacate.

often those with bad credit are looking to rent. It would be far less expensive for many of them to buy, but since they cannot qualify for a mortgage they have to rent, forcing landlords to relax normal standards.

In the five years that we owned Briarwood, our retention rate was so strong that for both apartments we wrote a total of only six rental contracts. Two of those six were to military couples with whom we became friends.

One of the perks we provide to our tenants is a monthly cleaning service. The cost of that amenity was covered by a small portion of the rent. The service included light cleaning (no dusting), with an emphasis on the bathrooms and kitchen. The benefit to the tenant is obvious, but as landlords, we maintain a sense of security that, whenever the tenant vacates, we do not run the risk of being left with a filthy mess.

After owning Briarwood for about 5 years, the New Jersey real estate market had peaked and was in the early stages of softening. One of our tenants, a single professional woman, sent us a letter informing us that in March she was relocating to another state for business purposes. When she first took the unit, she asked us to add a clause to her lease that would give her the freedom to vacate with a 60-day notice, if her company needed her elsewhere. She had an agreement with her firm, that if she needed to leave before the lease terminated, the company would pay her landlord $3,000 for breaking the lease. That money afforded us a two-month cushion to find another tenant.

> **Selling Tip:**
>
> When selling a duplex, it is ideal for at least one unit to be vacant in the event that a buyer might want to occupy one apartment themselves.

Shortly after we heard from her, the other tenants in the top unit sent us a letter informing us that they would not be renewing their lease. Learning that both units would become vacant within 30 days of each other made us think that maybe it was time to consider selling Briarwood.

When an investor is selling a duplex, it is ideal for at least one unit to be vacant in the event that a buyer might want to occupy one apartment themselves. The timing was perfect because spring and summer are the best times of the year to market real estate, especially in a resort area.

Gayle, the realtor who helped us with our Allenhurst purchase, was contacted to prepare a short-term, four-month listing. An ad was placed to rent only one of the units, with a plan to leave the second apartment vacant while seeking a buyer. By June, a Chinese man who was opening an Asian restaurant on the board-walk at the Belmar beach signed a lease to rent the lower unit. Because we were not totally certain that the Lord wanted the building sold, we decided that if we did not get a reasonable contract offer by the end of the summer, we would take the property off the market and find another tenant. In addition to our prayers, sometimes we try to determine God's will by circumstances as they unfold.

Labor Day came and up to that day there had been no offer to purchase. There were several showings but nothing more. When Gayle called to remind us that the listing was about to expire, Keith and I decided to extend the listing one more month. Due to the money Gayle and her company had invested in advertising, it would be more considerate if we listed for

> **Selling Note:**
>
> Generally, income properties take longer to sell than residential homes.

one more month, and the weather in Belmar was still beautiful in September. Generally, income properties take longer to sell than residential homes, so we were in agreement that another 30 days on the market would be wise.

Shortly after Labor Day, we got a call from Gayle informing us that she had just received a contract with a solid offer on Briarwood. The real estate market had so escalated during our five years of ownership, that we were able to list the property for $619,000, allowing plenty of room for negotiations. The offer came in at $579,000, certainly a fair price. Gayle encouraged us to seriously consider the contract and get back to her.

What was really interesting about the Buyers is that they were a Chinese couple who did not speak English. All translations were handled by their adult son. That got our attention.

What were the chances that several months earlier we would rent one of the units to a Chinese man with the potential to communicate with these new landlords? Believing that this was not a coincidence, we countered the offer at $589,000 and our Buyers accepted. Both Keith and I felt so incredibly blessed. The transaction went through without a hitch and we walked away with our second real estate windfall.

> **Buying Tip:**
>
> To make informed decisions, investors need to study their market areas before making offers.

After Briarwood was sold, we determined that we would put real estate investing on the back burner until the market returned to an upward swing. As the housing prices were slowly descending, it was becoming more prudent for people to buy than to rent. We stopped looking at real estate investment properties for about six years.

Lexington, SC

Fast forward to 2010. When foreclosures became plentiful, we started looking at real estate again. It was my desire to pay cash for a small house so that we could improve our monthly income and have an alternative place to live, should our life circumstances change.

On a Saturday evening in June, 2010, I was browsing the local Multiple Listing Service online to check out housing prices in Lexington, SC, a nearby community. (Chapter Eleven details our move to South Carolina.) Not long before, we made a low offer on a serious fixer and were outbid by someone planning to live in the house. Due to all the work that house needed, we were relieved when we were outbid by others. Since we had been looking for awhile, we had a pulse on the local market, which is very important when investing. In order to make informed decisions, investors need to study their market areas before making offers.

To my delight, I came across a 1550 sq. foot, two-story colonial with three bedrooms and two-and-a-half baths. The formal dining room, large living room with fireplace, one-car garage, huge fenced and land-scaped yard, large screened-in porch and a sizeable deck were features that would appeal to tenants. Because the property was in foreclosure, the asking price was only $94,900. I printed out the listing and showed it to Keith. He too was impressed, and we immediately made an appointment with our realtor, Denise Johnson, of *Coldwell Banker* in Irmo, SC.

Buying Note:

Another challenge with foreclosures is that banks can take weeks to respond to offers.

Often, foreclosures are trashed and restoring them can be costly. This house was different. As soon as we saw the good condition of this 22-year-old house, we knew we wanted to buy it. Normally we would not initially offer to pay the asking price however, the price had been lowered the day before I found the listing. Because two-story homes are often very popular, we wanted to make a deal with the bank as quickly as possible to avoid a potential bidding war. Another challenge with foreclosures is that banks can take weeks to respond to offers. In this case, the bank was quick to respond and within days the account managers had accepted our full price offer.

Since we were paying cash, the only contingency we had in our contract was a home inspection. No one purchasing any type of real estate, whether residential or commercial, should ever waive their right to a property inspection. It is also crucial to find a thor-ough and reputable house inspector. Ours advised us that the entire air-conditioning system was not functioning and was likely

Buying Tip:

Never waive your right to a property inspection!

86

too dated to repair. A new hot water heater had to be installed, along with a few other odds and ends that needed attention, including the painting of several rooms. We determined that installing some lattice on the porch would be a worthy investment so that little children and pets would not fall through the screens.

Foreclosure contracts always specify that the buyer is purchasing the property "As-Is" and the "Seller will make no repairs." That being said, as stated previously, Keith and I believe that sometimes it is worth asking for a price adjustment. We were under the impression from the listing that the AC was working since it was listed on the contract and we had no "Seller Disclosure" to the contrary.

When we found out that the AC was totally non-functional, we decided that we would try to get the bank to give us a price adjustment for the cost of a new unit. We knew it was a long shot, but because we were cash buyers, we thought it was worth a try. Within days, we had an answer back from the bank that they were willing to lower the price of the property to 90,900. This was a huge blessing because banks almost never renegotiate a foreclosure contract for any reason. It was our confirmation from the Lord that we were in His will with this purchase.

We then found a competent handyman on *Craig's List*. (Ever since I started to use *Craig's List* as a resource, we have been blessed with wonderful workers and helpers. One should be careful to get credible references when contacting strangers, but many reputable people advertise on *Craig's List*.) With his help, in a few months time, we were able to prepare the house to show to potential renters and by December of that year, we had our first tenants.

What is interesting about South Carolina is that taxes for a property vary, depending on whether or not it is your personal residence or an income-producing property. On this Lexington house for example, if we were to live there ourselves, our annual taxes would be less than $700. As an income property, the annual taxes jump up to almost $3,000. The home owner's insurance is about $60 per-month and, of course, we needed to conserve some money for repairs. Thankfully, we were able to rent the house for $1100 per month, giving us a very nice return on our investment.

Real estate investing for income is not for the 'faint of heart.' Many issues can arise that are both unforeseen and unfortunate. Anticipation of each purchase has caused us feelings of apprehension and we had all the concerns that most people experience. We wondered: Should we risk our money? Will our tenants be responsible? Will the challenges be worth the income? Will we regret this purchase? While these are all very legitimate concerns, if real estate investing is God's will for one's life, the potential challenges should not paralyze people with fear.

We pray over each of our purchases diligently and literally beg God to not let us make a mistake. We have always been willing to walk away if we don't have clear direction from Him. We never choose an income property that we would not be willing to live in ourselves. Once all the homework is complete, a leap of faith is necessary to be able to move forward.

Earlier I mentioned the importance of using an agency for credit and criminal checks. While to date we have not regretted any of our real estate investments, we did relax our standards in choosing non-credit worthy tenants for our Lexington rental property. After reviewing the credit reports of the prospective tenants, Keith and I made a decision to give those applicants a chance to redeem themselves after dealing with the setbacks of a previous job loss. The couple seemed nice enough and gave us a copy of a letter from the new boss on company letterhead confirming a very nice starting salary. We thought God wanted us to take a chance on them and rent them our house in spite of their less than stellar record. And so we did.

> **Investing Tip:**
>
> We never choose an income property that we would not be willing to live in ourselves.

The tenants paid rent monthly for the first year, although sometimes late, and signed a lease for the second year. In the ninth month of the second year, they simply stopped paying rent and would not move out for two months. Damages to the screened porch and wall-to-wall carpeting exceeded their $1100 security deposit.

Keith and I then decided that we would put the Lexington house up for sale to get our cash back out of that investment. Though I had months worth of work to give the whole house a facelift, I agreed with Keith that it was time to sell.

In the meantime, our son Sean was actively looking to purchase a house in Lexington in the price range of our investment house. Often while I was painting there, I was praying that the Lord would inspire Sean to choose our house. I determined that I would not try to sell it to him and that buying it would have to be his idea.

One night Sean came to us and told us that he thought the Lord might want him to buy our house. We arranged a tour and Sean decided that our investment property would be perfect for him and our grandson, Tyler.

As God would have it, one of our neighbors, was in the process of downsizing and moving about the same time that Sean was planning to move into the Lexington house. They offered him furniture, a washer and dryer and everything he needed to set up a kitchen!

Our other neighbors had furniture from their previous home that they were looking to give away as well. Between the two families, Sean's house is almost entirely furnished with no cost to him! Had our tenants not left our property pre-maturely, the timing for all the free furniture would have been way off, along with Sean's timetable for moving.

Even though our former tenants owe us money, which we know we will never see, the Lord had a wonderful plan for that house all along. I am so grateful that we are keeping that property in the family because I am able to continue to appreciate the fruits of my labor while Sean and Tyler live in a warm and inviting home.

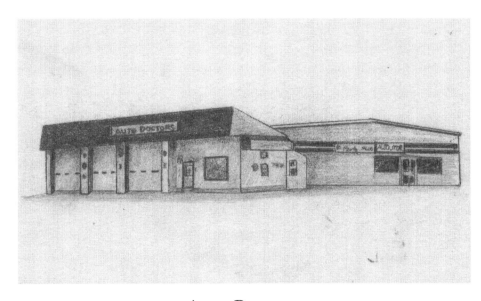

AUTO DOCTORS

Chapter Eight

OUR SUCCESSFUL BUSINESS & PROPERTY

*I*n January of 2007, while still in Wilmington, we hosted a neighborhood house party to ring in the New Year. A few months prior to the party, Keith talked about selling his business, *Townsend Motor World T/A Auto Doctors,* in Delaware. He was working long hours and felt he didn't have enough quality time with his family, especially when the grandchildren came to town. Keith felt ready for a change and hoped that he might find a business to purchase that would be large enough to include our son, Sean. *Auto Doctors* paid us well while we owned it, but we could not afford to add Sean to the payroll.

One of our neighbors at the party was a commercial real estate broker. Dave and Keith talked briefly about Dave's career in commercial properties. Keith began to wonder if Dave might be able to help us sell our company once we determined it was time to do so. After the party, we were hopeful that our neighbor could be our 'go to guy,' someone in the industry who we could trust. Time would tell.

By the end of January, we did make the decision to sell. Often, selling a service center with a parts store, including the building, takes a very long time. There are few buyers because most of those who would be interested may not have the means to make such a large purchase.

Our asking price for the business and the building combined was $950,000, a total that was determined after we asked Dave to come to Townsend and evaluate the property. He took photos and put together a marketing packet. However, Dave did not list the property because his office and focus was in Pennsylvania not Delaware. We set the marketing packet aside for weeks without moving forward, or making any attempts to list.

Sometime in March, Keith received an unexpected phone call from Dave to tell us that he had a broker friend in Delaware who might have a buyer for *Auto Doctors*. The broker friend called Keith explaining that his client needed to make a 1031-Exchange purchase. (Tax professionals can explain such transactions.)

The broker made an appointment to show the business to his client. The client then came back by himself, without a professional building inspector, to make his own inspection. After approving the building and looking at the books, Keith was offered the full asking price without any counter offers.

Due to the rise in the real estate industry from the time that we bought the building until the sale, we accumulated significant equity. The contract was drawn up and signed with a closing date of July 19, 2007. From beginning to end the whole negotiation period took only about a month. Only God could have orchestrated such an easy sale. In July of the same year we would walk away with another $300,000 in equity, with thankful hearts that the transactions moved along so quickly.

A Life-Changing Accident

By the time the decision had been made to sell *Auto Doctors*, Sean was separated from his wife and in the process of a divorce.

Together they had a two-year-old son, Tyler, whom Sean adored. Keith determined that we could search Delaware, Southern Jersey and the Philadelphia area of Pennsylvania for another company. As long as Sean could be within a two hour driving distance to see Tyler for visitations, we had tri-state options.

We spent a lot of time at the bizbuysell.com website looking for a company with enough cash flow to support two families. Keith's desire was to get out of the car industry, but he did not discount auto-related companies. We were open to all types of businesses and inquired about everything from cell phone companies to watermelon purveyors.

Two weeks before the closing on *Auto Doctors* at 1 a.m. in the morning of July 5th, we received a startling phone call, waking us from a deep sleep. It was Sean, in a voice of disbelief, telling us that his ex-wife drowned in a boating accident, less than six-hours earlier. His son Tyler had been on the boat as well but was unharmed and waiting at the hospital for Sean to pick him up. By God's amazing grace, Tyler, only two-and-a-half-years old, survived because of his life jacket and the quick thinking of the captain who got the children out of the water and set them on top of the capsized 18' boat.

Tyler and his mother had been boating with four other adults and his cousin to see the fireworks from the water. Five-foot waves, 35 mph winds and impending rain influenced the official's decision to cancel the fireworks. Almost no other boats were out, except one pontoon boat. The captain of the pontoon and his guest witnessed the accident and immediately came to the rescue. Ty's mother was the only one who drowned, and though they attempted CPR, it is believed she died before arriving at the hospital.

After Keith hung up and shared the news with me, I knew in my spirit that my life was about to change dramatically and it took me a long time to fall back asleep. I could see the Delaware River from my side of the bed. I lay still as I watched the freighters for hours going back and forth across the water while praying prayers of gratitude that the Lord spared Tyler's life, and longing for sleep to come back over me so that I would not have to think about tomorrow, or the days ahead.

When we went to New Jersey the next day to be with Sean and Tyler, Keith asked Sean what he needed. Sean's reply was, "A new address." At the time Sean was living with his maternal grandmother as his divorce had only been final for one week prior to the accident. He had not even begun to rebuild his life at that point. Now there would be no sharing of custody, as Sean had full responsibility for his son. It was the appropriate time to make major changes.

We suggested that Sean quit his job in central New Jersey and move into The Villa with us. Our *Auto Doctors* closing was only a few weeks away. It would be easier for Keith and Sean to look at alternative business options with Sean nearby, and we knew Sean would need some help with Tyler. Ty had just witnessed the death of his mother, so we knew the emotional trauma for a toddler was bound to manifest itself in due time.

Overnight, Sean suddenly had the freedom to move anywhere with Tyler. There were no laws forcing a stay in New Jersey or anywhere in the Northeast for that matter. Sean and Ty moved into our newly-designated third bedroom on the ground floor of the Villa and I moved my desk and filing cabinet into the adjoining furnace room. This would have to be a temporary set up, but at least we all had our own space. Now it was time to figure out where we would move from there. This business search continued and expanded.

Heading South

Our adopted son Joey and his wife, Nicole, were living in Lexington, South Carolina where Joey was employed with the Richland County Sherriff's Department. When I first came down to visit Joey and Nicole, Keith still owned *Auto Doctors* and couldn't get away. Joey drove me around the Columbia area and took me over the Lake Murray Dam. When I saw Lake Murray for the first time, I knew Keith would someday love to own a piece of property on the lake if that were ever possible. Now that we could expand our search, we began to look for a company in South Carolina, where we were confident we would all enjoy living.

With Sean and Tyler living with us, it soon became abundantly clear that we needed to find a larger home. In Delaware, the price tag for homes expansive enough for the four of us, were in the $400,000 to $600,000 range. We determined we could get a lot more for our money by relocating to the South where housing prices and taxes were considerably lower.

A month after Sean and Ty moved into our townhouse, the four of us headed to South Carolina for business meetings and house hunting. As I expected, Keith was enamored with Lake Murray and wanted to look at real estate during our visit. It was amazing to us how much house we could purchase for $500,000 with extremely low property taxes. We looked at two houses on the lake, and numerous large homes in the town of Lexington.

Our heart's desire was to find an affordable home on Lake Murray. We returned to Wilmington believing that a move to South Carolina could be a good choice for our family, but we would need time to consider all aspects before making such a radical relocation.

Keith and Sean continued to analyze companies in the Northeast as well as in South Carolina. We prayed for wisdom daily, especially regarding the purchase of another company. I spent time on the computer looking at South Carolina real estate. While searching online in early October, I found a Lake Murray *short sale* that looked like an amazing house. Keith was impressed as well. We decided to go for it and put The Villa on the market.

Because The Villa was so impressive, within a few months we had a buyer and negotiated a price of $300,000. However, Christian had doubts about whether the property would appraise for that amount. The market had begun to soften and appraisers were being much more conservative with their numbers. We had the most amenities of all the townhouses in our development, making it the most valuable.

Normally, it is not ideal to own the most expensive house on the block. However, there are times when people spend more on renovations than they can recoup, simply because they can. Over-investing is really a bad idea if, when selling, the owner will lose money invested. Being the savvy realtor that he is, Christian's discernment about the appraisal was exactly right. The Villa was valued at only $291,000, making that the new sale price.

A good equity cushion as a result of our great original purchase price made The Villa another real estate success for us. Savvy investors understand that their money is made when the property is purchased. It is crucial to buy the real estate at a reasonable price so that when the time comes to sell, there has been ample time for equity growth.

By the end of January, 2008 The Villa was sold and we were headed south with Sean, Tyler, our cat Misha and an Allied 18-wheeler with all our earthly possessions. We went in faith because our residential property had not yet been secured, nor were we certain of what company we would buy. We were confident the Lord had a plan that He would reveal in His time.

We know we were appropriately named when we read Genesis 12:1, "The Lord said to Abram, 'Go to the land I will show you.'"

And the Abrams went . . . wondering.

THE FORECLOSURE

Chapter Nine

THE FORECLOSURE PROPERTY FOR OUR GROWING FAMILY

*O*ur daughter Kristin and son-in-law Paul Rizzo lived in five homes since the day they got married. Each home came with a financial blessing.

Their first post-wedding abode was a cozy two-bedroom duplex in Garfield, New Jersey. The property was owned by a close family friend who gave the Rizzo's a discounted monthly rental of $500 for a $900 value. It was at this time in their lives that Paul and Kristin were working diligently to get out of debt from each of their previous marriages. We were proud of their decision to pay off all credit card debt in order to achieve the goal of financial freedom.

Two years later, the Rizzos had the opportunity to move into Kristin's deceased grandmother's home in the prestigious borough of Ho-Ho-Kus, New Jersey. The old fashioned, two-bedroom cottage featured a large fieldstone fireplace in the living room with hardwood floors throughout. The small sun room, also boasting field stones, had elongated windows to the ceiling which allowed the outdoors in. The property, while in desperate need of a renovation, was very charming and held great sentimental value to our daughter.

Kristin had an agreement with her Dad who inherited the house, that in lieu of traditional rent, she and Paul would hire someone to remodel the tiny bathroom and pay the contractor directly. They lived in the house for only ten months, incurring a cost of $4,000 for the bath repairs, essentially paying only $400 per month in 'rent' plus the utilities. That was a grand bargain for a rental property worth $1200 per month.

During their time in Ho-Ho-Kus, Paul and Kristin reasoned that for the long term, they should prayerfully consider relocating to a more affordable region of the Country. Looking online, they found an open position for a principal of a parochial elementary school in *Southern Pines*, North Carolina. At the time, Paul was serving as the principal of a New Jersey Catholic elementary school. With the ability to preview real estate on the Internet, the Rizzos could plainly see that moving south could make their dream of home ownership a reality.

Once Paul had the job offer, they took a spring weekend and headed to North Carolina to look for a house. In 2004, there was not an abundance of properties in their price range, so the search was quickly narrowed down to just two houses. The one they chose was wonderful, but in need of some updating.

The all-brick ranch was situated second to the last house on a dead end street. The unique large lot had little grass, but plenty of lush bushes and trees, with a small creek bordering the backyard. A massive 27x14-foot, three-season screened porch ran across the back of the house, giving one the sense of being enveloped by nature.

Three large bedrooms, each with oversized closets, two-and-a-half baths, and an appealing open floor plan for the living room and dining room areas, made this property outstanding. The oversized two-car garage was an added bonus, all for only $122,000 with a $3,000 carpet allowance. The property taxes on this spacious 1800-square-foot custom home were less than $1,000 annually.

This property in Aberdeen, NC, was a great find and an opportunity to build equity over a four-plus year period of time. An acceptable offer was made and they headed back to Jersey to pack.

Late in June, Kristin and Paul left family and friends in the northeast and moved south to begin their new life. They both love the NY metropolitan area, but knew that they would have to be content with visiting as often as possible. Though they've left portions of their hearts in the Northeast, they love the life they are making in North Carolina. Kristin says, "New Jersey will always be home." But in North Carolina they now are able to experience southern blessings.

Eventually Paul left private Catholic education after his personal decision to leave the Roman Catholic Church. He found work as a high school history teacher and football coach in the local public education system. The county gave Paul credit for his years in private education. Thankfully, he did not have to start at the bottom of the pay scale when he made the switch.

Paul always enjoys working with teenagers. He and a colleague designed an Ambassador's Program to encourage under-privileged teens to become involved in their communities. We are very proud of his many accomplishments.

Another educational chapter began in August of 2013 as Paul has been hired as the new Campus Director for Covenant Prep, a private University Model Classical Christian School in Carthage, NC. Paul, Kristin and other concerned parents founded the school with the support and help of New Covenant Fellowship Christian Church.

This unique model is a much needed educational option for parents who want to home school but also understand the benefits of having a physical location with quality teachers to support them in educating their children several days a week. This scholastic opportunity also helps enhance socialization for the children. Many who have previously felt inadequate to home school see the University Model as a viable choice for their children. (For more information: www.covenantprep.com)

Sell and Rent?

While living in Aberdeen, Kristin and Paul had two children, Angelina, and Landon. The U.S. economy was in a tail spin and the Rizzos had concerns about declining values in the housing market. They prayed and decided to put their home up for sale to see what might happen.

Carolyn Ragone, owner and broker of Carolyn Ragone Real Estate, LLC suggested they start at $189,000. Paul and Kristin wisely began to discuss the idea of renting should their house sell, so they could ride out the downturn and not end up overpaying for their next house. Implementing a rental situation would ultimately require two moves, but it would not prove prudent to buy in a volatile market.

In June, military friends from the Rizzo's church decided they wanted to rent out their home as they were soon to leave Southern Pines for another tour-of-duty. These friends felt that the Lord wanted them to offer their home for a greatly reduced rent so that they could bless another family that needed a financial break. Word got out at church that they would be looking for qualified tenants.

Since Landon's birth, Kristin could not maintain a high level of commitment to her full time career as a *Southern Living at Home* Director. She had been earning a significant second income during almost seven years of being a top producer in sales for her company. In addition, Kristin earned almost all the exotic, all-expense-paid trips that *Southern Living at Home* offered. However, beginning in 2009, the logistics of marketing through home parties no longer worked well for their family and an opportunity to lighten their financial load would be a wonderful blessing.

Early in June, when the Rizzo's found out about the Smith's (their friends from church) rental opportunity, Kristin called for details and to express an interest. Though their Aberdeen house had not yet sold, they figured it would not hurt to tour the rental house and see if it could be a good fit for their family.

I happened to be visiting the day of the appointment and was invited to go along. Being the real estate junkie that I am, I was thrilled to be included. Our children have been gracious about our input in the matters of real estate and we are grateful for their respect.

The Smith's home, a spacious 1930's California-type bungalow in Southern Pines was warm and welcoming. From the craftsman-style front door, and throughout, it was a home that made you want to stay. Two highlights of the large living room were the beamed, vaulted, wood ceiling and a massive fieldstone fireplace on the focal wall. Hardwoods were the floors of choice throughout the original portion of the house. A well-appropriated addition including a sun room and a guest suite with a private bath, was a perfect place for in-laws. Small-paned, shuttered windows throughout the entire house insured a seamless connection between the original house and the not-so-recent addition. Though there were only two bedrooms in the main portion of the house, they were large, and Kristin and Paul determined that Angelina and Landon could share a room for the duration of the rental.

The Smiths were asking only $650 per month, in a town that could have commanded $1100 or more for that property. The new landlords were also willing to write a two-year lease if needed. This rental would be extremely helpful to Kristin and Paul, but they still had a house to sell in order to make it work. The Smiths were willing to wait until the first weekend in August for an answer. If the Rizzos did not sell by then, the Smiths would seek other tenants.

At that point, it was clear that Kristin and Paul would need to lower the asking price of their house in order to move the sale along. They had already dropped $10,000 off the original asking price, but after prayerful consideration and consultation with Carolyn, they decided on $165,000 with the hope of facilitating a quick sale. Their prayer was that if God wanted them to sell and move to the Southern Pines rental, He would send a buyer. If He didn't send a buyer, they would stay put in Aberdeen and take their house off the market.

June and July passed without an offer. The deadline to commit to the Smiths was Monday August 3. On Friday, July 31, a realtor brought a potential buyer. He was in the military, soon to be stationed at Fort Bragg. The young man had only the weekend to make a decision. He really liked the house and forwarded photos to his pregnant wife, who was impressed with what she could see via modern technology.

On Saturday, the potential buyer stopped by the house to meet the Rizzos, not to get out of paying a commission, but to get more information about the property. He and Paul bonded right away because they had a lot in common.

The next day—the last day to make a sale before having to contact the Smiths, Carolyn came by with an offer. It was lower than what Kristin and Paul had hoped, but the buyers told the realtor that they were coming in with their best offer of $157,000. They said it was at the top of their budget and hoped the Rizzos were not offended. Feeling strongly that this was the family God sent to purchase their home, Paul and Kristin agreed to the offer and by the end of the day had a contract signed by both parties. God is never late, but sometimes seems to test us up to our deadlines.

The Move

A mid-September closing was scheduled and a rental contract with the Smiths was signed, with an agreement that Kristin and Paul could have a key to move personal belongings into the rental property before the official contract date of September 1, 2009.

Sheila and Brian Theune, close friends of the Rizzos, graciously offered to orchestrate the move from Aberdeen to Southern Pines. Sheila told Kristin not to worry, because their church members always help each other when needed. Paul and Kristin were fairly new

> God is never late, but sometimes seems to test us up to our deadlines.

attendees at *Sandhills Presbyterian Church* and were unfamiliar with the generosity of their fellow believers.

It is important to note the benefits of being part of a group of people who worship together, and share the common belief that the Lord wants us to have a servant's heart.

Therefore, as we have opportunity, let us do good to all people, especially to those who belong to the family of believers.
Galatians 6:10

Serve one another in love. The entire law is summed up in a single command: 'Love your neighbor as yourself.'
Galatians 5:13b &14

The Rizzos could not have imagined the magnitude of the help they were about to receive, not only from Sheila and Brian, but from others in the church who were beckoned to help one Saturday to move the furniture and multiple boxes. While I was able to come up for a few days to help with the children and some packing, it was Sheila who helped Kristin pack the whole house. Paul had a summer job and was limited in what he could do.

The move was made without the benefit of a conventional moving truck or box truck rental. Sheila's SUV and trailer, along with another church friend's vehicle and trailer, handled the bulk of the move. Prior to that day Sheila had already made multiple trips back and forth, and, following that day, she continued until everything had been moved from Aberdeen to Southern Pines. I doubt that I have ever seen a friend work that hard for another out of a heart of love and compassion.

> It is important to note the benefits of being part of a group of people who worship together, and share the common belief that the Lord wants us to have a servant's heart.

Without Sheila's ability to organize and persevere, moving for Kristin and Paul would have been very expensive and overwhelming.

Another Baby

While living in the rental, Kristin became pregnant with their third baby, Gianna. Once Gianna came into the world, the rental was no longer large enough for the growing Rizzo family. As God would have it, shortly after the one-year lease had expired, the Smiths had a major change in their lives and indicated they would need to raise the rent to $950 per month by the end of the calendar year. In the meantime, they would continue to rent to Paul and Kristin at the lower rate with a month-to-month contract, giving the Rizzos time to find another place to live. Paul and Kristin did not want to pay that higher rent when they could buy a house for the same money.

The search was on for a house purchase as the Rizzos knew that one more move was all they could handle. As much as they enjoyed living in Southern Pines it was a bit pricey, so they extended their search into neighboring towns. By this time, being more active in their church, they didn't want to move too far away from the area. Realtor Carolyn Ragone showed them many houses within 15 minutes of the church, but Paul and Kristin were not motivated to make an offer on homes that lacked the combination of appeal and affordability.

The Rizzos decided to expand their search to the Seven Lakes area of North Carolina which had originally been designed as a resort community. It is about 25 minutes from their church, but closer to Paul's school. The amenities for Seven Lakes, a gated community include: an Olympic-sized swimming pool, tennis courts, a club house, horseback riding and a golf course surrounded by lovely custom-built homes.

Kristin asked Carolyn to send her all the Seven Lakes properties that were on the market and the Rizzos picked out the ones they thought might work for their family. Some were too small, others had unsuitable floor plans and the most spacious one was dingy and musty. Discouraged and wondering what could possibly be God's plan, they went back to the listings to be sure they had not missed anything.

Indeed, one had been overlooked, most likely because the $174,900 price tag was higher than the homes previously under consideration. But there it was: a stunning foreclosure with all the space the Rizzos could have hoped for on a lovely, large corner lot close to the golf course. The stately, two-story, 2500-square-foot home with four bedrooms, a nursery and two-and-a-half baths was worthy of at least a tour. Kristin set up an appointment with Carolyn for the next day.

The photos in the listing did not do the house justice. It was bright and airy with casement windows throughout. The large eat-in kitchen with granite countertops and wood-stained cabinetry, opened to the family room with a brick, raised-hearth fireplace on one side, and to a sun room in the back, perfect for home-schooling. A formal dining room and spacious living room were perfect for entertaining. With the exception of the first floor guest room, the other bedrooms made up the second floor. This could be the perfect home for the Rizzo family.

When Kristin and Paul got in the van after their house tour, Paul took a towellete out of the diaper bag and started wiping Kristin's chin. When she asked him what he was doing, Paul responded, "I am wiping away all the drool coming from your mouth." Kristin got a real belly laugh out of that. After a short time of private conversation, they called Carolyn and asked her to prepare a contract for the foreclosure in Seven Lakes.

The first offer was low at $150,000. The asking price on the house was below the appraised value, making the initial offering unlikely for acceptance and so it was refused. The final negotiated price was $170,000, subject to a house inspection.

The reason that the Rizzos were able to afford a house for $170,000 is because the interest rates had come down to an all-time low of 4%. Had the rate been a percentage point higher, that house would have been out of reach for their budget. God's timing was perfect. At closing, Paul and Kristin paid only $168,000 because they requested and were granted a $2,000 price reduction due to some needed septic repairs. As noted previously, even foreclosures are not *always* strictly "As-Is" sales.

> **Financial blessings often come to us when we are obedient to the Lord and give back to Him the portion He requires of us.**

The deal was sealed and the closing date set for mid-November. Now it was time to pack up again, only this time there were *three* children and all their 'stuff'. Again, many dear friends from *Sandhills Presbyterian Church* came to the rescue.

One close friend, Mark Ivy, offered the use of his large box truck and others came through with their vans. Many people jumped in to help, including the pastor of the church who also lives in the Seven Lakes neighborhood. Multiple trips between Southern Pines and Seven Lakes eventually transferred all the family's belongings. There were so many friends who helped; they cannot all be listed here.

The kindness and sacrifices of the Rizzo's friends were a wonderful witness to all who know them. I made several trips up from South Carolina to help pack, and then Keith and I went up together for the weekend after celebrating Thanksgiving at home with our other children. How thankful we were to see the new space that Kristin and Paul now owned. If their house on such a beautiful and large lot in Seven Lakes was located in many parts of New Jersey, it would cost more than a half-million dollars, not to mention the added expense of high property taxes. Moving south has been worth the effort for this young family.

> **Our motivation to give should not be for the purpose of receiving, but purely to honor the One who sustains us every hour of every day of life.**

How grateful Keith and I will always be to the friends from their church who loved on our children and grandchildren. Since the move into the Seven Lakes foreclosure, the Lord has blessed Kristin and Paul with their fourth child, Thorin. Clearly the Rizzo family needed all the space they now possess.

Reasons for Blessings

Financial blessings often come to us when we are obedient to the Lord and give back to Him the portion He requires of us.

> *A tithe of everything from the land, whether grain*
> *from the soil or fruit from the trees, belongs to*
> *the Lord, it is holy to the Lord.*
> Leviticus 27:30

> *Bring the whole tithe into the storehouse, that there may*
> *be food in my house. 'Test me in this,' says the Lord*
> *Almighty, 'and see if I will not throw open*
> *the floodgates of heaven and pour out so*
> *much blessing that you will not have*
> *room enough for it.'*
> Malachi 3:10

There are many ways in which we are blessed. Blessings come to us in many forms, often more than just money, and can include health, relationships with people and pets, work, good attitudes, a zest for life, and the list goes on. Our motivation to give should not be for the purpose of receiving, but purely to honor the One who sustains us every hour of every

> Initially, we need to give to God out of obedience, even if our hearts and minds are struggling. The more we are obedient, the more we trust, and the easier it becomes to give with enthusiasm.

day of life. He asks us to give back to Him only a tithe—10 percent—and allows us to manage the other 90 percent as we see fit. Not only do we get to keep most of our income (though the government often takes more than it should), but then He promises to bless us when we are obedient.

We are so grateful that our children are following our lead, as we have followed the lead of our parents, and have learned to tithe at relatively young ages. Kristin and Paul worked their way up to giving ten percent as the Lord increased their faith. Tithing is a walk of faith, especially when one is not used to taking ten out of every one hundred dollars and giving it away.

I believe that initially, we need to give to God out of obedience, even if our hearts and minds are struggling. The more we are obedient, the more we trust and the easier it becomes to give with enthusiasm. Eventually, giving generously and not holding too tightly to our belongings is liberating and brings us great joy.

It is important that we maintain a theological balance in our approach to blessings. A highly recommended and balanced book on giving is *The Blessed Life* by Robert Morris. In it, he clearly outlines both the blessing and joy that comes from giving when we follow God's financial plan for His people. Keith and I do not believe that everyone was meant to have a lot of money. God knows who will handle it well, and who will not. We think, however, in an effort to keep from being out of balance with a 'prosperity gospel' mindset, sometimes believers miss out on blessings the Lord has in store for them. A balanced outlook on *prosperity* is vital to a liberating walk with the Lord.

Sometimes real estate choices, even when prayed over, can present challenges with purpose. Our daughter Tara and son-in-law Mike Raymo would experience intense stress in their second home. This book would not be complete without Tara's reflections on the home that depleted their bank account.

TEXAS CHALLENGE

Chapter Ten

A CHARACTER-BUILDING PROPERTY

When our daughter, Tara Raymo, found out I was writing a book about seeing God's hand in real estate transactions, she offered to write the incredibly challenging experience she and her husband Mike had when they purchased an older house in Temple, Texas. There is much for us to learn, so this is the Raymo story in Tara's own words …

I once read a quote that went like this, "God is more concerned about our character than about our comfort. He is more interested in making us holy rather than happy." I copied these words onto a piece of paper and taped it to my kitchen window so that I would be reminded during my daily dish duties. Thankfully, I had much time to commit

> The physical foundation of our home is less important to Him than the foundation upon which we build our hopes, loyalties and, most importantly, our souls.

that statement to memory, as it has undeniably proven true for us throughout our relocation.

In our minds, a home should be a place of comfort, rest and happiness. Certainly, the home improvement reality television shows are constantly striving to create that type of atmosphere for homeowners. Although it is fun to watch those programs, God wants us to be tuned into His channel. He's got credentials in interior design all right, but it's not the type that we're typically fond of. His priority is the interior design of our hearts and not our dining room.

The physical foundation of our home is less important to Him than the foundation upon which we build our hopes, loyalties and, most importantly, our souls. Repairing a leaky sewer pipe doesn't bring our Heavenly Father nearly as much joy, as does altering what is flowing in and out of our lives. Weak and crumbling walls around our houses are but a mere nuisance compared to the damage caused by walls we wrongly construct to keep Him at a "safe" distance.

While the Lord is completely capable of handling all of these exterior property management issues, His delight is to develop a place of comfort, rest and happiness inside of us. He promises the design process will last a lifetime and often be unpleasant, but will lead to a better place for our hearts to dwell because He'll be found in every room. After all, "Home is where the heart is," and I want mine to be with Jesus!

Let the Lessons Begin

If time and children haven't aged you, you can be sure buying an older home in one weekend will! Our first one-weekend real estate purchase worked out just fine, but that house was half as old as the next. The second time around didn't go quite as smoothly.

Following the usual inspection, we happily purchased a sixty-year-old stone house with a cottage-like feel, in an established neighborhood with mature trees. It had the original paned glass windows, built-in ironing board, telephone wall niche, as well as extra features unique to the 1950s era. The ceilings in the bathroom showers were rather low, giving my husband about two inches of clearance above him, which earned it the name, "Hobbit-House." For all intents and purposes, it was a cozy home with a nice floor-plan, lots of space, and in need of some TLC. A few updates/revi-sions, such as raising shower height, fixing sprinkler heads and painting vintage pink cabinets were also needed. Unbeknownst to us, the house was actually more trouble than we bargained for. It didn't take too long to discover that this spacious bungalow would become a noose around our necks. Our idea of a seamless transition from one home to another was *not* going to happen.

It all started in the garage. So much goes on in that dreadful place. You know, empty boxes, strange tools that nobody knows how to use, antique photos of scary-looking people, stuff left over from the previous owners and many more surprises awaiting unsuspecting visitors. On the flipside, a garage is a man's pride and joy.

Naturally, my husband wanted to transform the place into a haven of functional storage space for, wouldn't you know: cars and lawn equipment. His plan was to liven it up with a fresh coat of paint to give it that "clean" feeling. There were also visions of painting the concrete floor, but those were quickly overshadowed by more pressing issues. Since the walls were in bad shape with lots of peeling paint, we set to work vigor-

> **Remodeling Note:**
>
> A federal government regulation implemented April 22, 2010, requires all contractors working on a home with lead paint to be certified and possess a license.

ously prepping and sanding them. A few hours passed as our two young boys, Samuel and Hudson, patiently waited with eager hands to help while we continued on. We soon realized our efforts were insufficient without professional assistance, as the task was too great and the results slow-going. Suddenly, in the midst of paint dust whirl-ing in the air, the thought occurred to us that due to the age of the home, we could be disrupting lead paint and breathing it in.

Taking a break from the August heat and possible lead particles in the garage, we moved inside to call a painter. After listening to our situation, this particular painter informed us of a new federal government regulation legislated on April 22, 2010, which requires all contractors working on a home with lead paint to be certified and possess a license. If caught without such things, they could face significant fines. Work guidelines and requirements are also very strict under the new law, making the contractors work much more tedious and laborious. Thus, he was not legally authorized to work on our home if it had lead-based paint. We were referred to one of the few painters in the area who held this certification and, as quickly as possible, we ran out to grab a bite to eat and pick up a do-it-yourself lead test kit.

With racing hearts and sweaty palms, we nervously awaited the results of the test kit, like we were taking a pregnancy test—even the color indicator was pink. Certain areas turned pink immediately, while others took a little longer

> God is always in control of timing.

but, sure enough, it was positive. At that point, we knew for sure what we should have discovered prior to buying the house.

Of course, our view is much clearer in retrospect, but somehow, it had all escaped us. The situation was very ominous, as our entire house was coated with chipping and peeling lead paint, including the kitchen and bathroom cabinetry and all windows. Had it been contained and in good condition, it would not have been such a problem. Our windows were the worst, with chips all over the floor and more ready to fall off. We simply didn't have the man-power, time, or equipment necessary to perform the task ourselves.

We quickly called the certified painter, and he came over on a Sunday after church to speak with us about it. It was determined that his crew would be more efficient *without* our belongings in the home, while they worked to get it fixed up. He also informed us that the lead paint law had been relaxed for the following few months to allow time for contractors to obtain these certifications.

In light of what we were facing, this was a huge blessing that we had to really strive to appreciate. The Lord in His mercy, allowed for a federal reprieve just in time for our work to be completed. The law was only relaxed from the summer until the end of December 2010, which gave them the amount of time they needed. God is always in control of timing.

Hours after meeting with the painter in Temple, we were driving back to our home in Houston to greet our movers early the next morning. Without much warning, we were scrambling around to find a climate-controlled storage facility for approximately 12,000 lbs. of

> There is a serenity that comes to children when they can see past their parent's inability to change a situation and focus on what Jesus is able to do.

'stuff', as well as a place to live for the next three months during our displacement.

It was a chaotic time, but considering our predicament, the Lord kept us rather calm through it all. Miraculously, we called a climate-controlled storage facility in town that had three units close together and available for us the day we needed them. We would have just enough space to fit everything.

Paper Plates & Pools

The next hurdle was to locate a place to rent for only three months, which was not readily available in a small central Texas town. Rentals were at a minimum and we were unsuccessful in finding anything before we actually moved. Fortunately, Mike had saved up some Marriot points from travel with his former employer, so we had a one-week free stay at a hotel.

Our boys thought the hotel with the pool was cool, and even in the midst of the confusion and uncertainty, they were calm and relaxed. They had already seen us cry more times in that one weekend than they had probably seen their whole lives, but despite all that, they managed to maintain their composure. Our youngest son actually referred to our new home as, "The House of Tears" since we shed them practically every time we walked in.

We take no credit for Samuel and Hudson's demeanor, nor give them credit for it, but do attribute it to two reasons. The boys had seen from the start that when we didn't know what to do, we ran to the One who did. There is a serenity that comes to children when they can see past their parent's inability to change a situation and focus on what Jesus is able to do. Also paramount in their coping skills was the fact that through it all, we were always together as a family. Sadly, togetherness is a concept that our society has lost, but it was a huge factor for our foursome in a time of crisis.

During our week-long hotel stay, our real estate agent located only two rental options for us. The first was not the greatest, but the second provided as clean and comfortable a space as possible, considering we'd be living out of suitcases and sleeping on air mattresses for three months. Our family enjoys camping, so at least we had a frame of reference for these sparse accommodations.

The next day we not only moved out of the hotel and into our rental, but Mike started working for a new company. The first day on a job is stressful enough, but adding all these living arrangements to the mix made it all the more challenging. God carried him through that also.

Mike not only did well, but totally impressed the management. He was promoted only two months later while we were still in transition. Mike's work load and salary increased, and we were very thankful for the extra income to help cover more of our sudden renovation expenses.

It's the Little Things

Thankfully, we had access to our storage units in order to pull out a few amenities that were not included with our rental, such as our tiny refrigerator, and, after too many trips to the laundry mat, our washer and dryer. Another blessing was the ability to transport these appliances as our vehicles were not big enough to load them up. The storage facility had a free truck usage program for all their renters, which was an enormous help to us. Mike even threw a small couch in the truck as a bonus.

Something as simple as hooking up the dryer just had to be difficult for my sweet husband. Unfortunately, the plug did not correspond to the outlet receptacle. Just because we had "bigger" issues to contend with, didn't mean that we were free from the "little" issues that can be so irritating. There were many of those irritants along our journey, such as a nail in our tire, indoor ants, locking ourselves out of our rental, leaky air mattresses, a cracked tooth, illnesses and more.

At times it seemed as if we couldn't make it through one more day without something that felt catastrophic happening to us. These weren't large problems at all, but they just seemed larger than life because they kept coming one after another.

The feelings we had during this time remind me of growing up on the Jersey Shore enjoying the summer ocean water, when the waves would come knock me down. Just when I would get up and get a footing, the next wave would come knock me down again. Too much of that turned tiresome very quickly. However, I never stayed down, because God always gave, and continues to give, just enough respite and strength to get me back up again. Every day, here on earth in our momentary troubles, He keeps picking us up.

Finding a General Contractor

The painter we met that Sunday recommended his friend, a general contractor, to coordinate all the renovations to include patching walls, new windows throughout, adding doorways, raising shower stalls, all new countertops and cabinets, paint, etc. Prior to our move, we had already determined that I would home school our two boys beginning with the fall semester. Since school was just about to start, a GC sounded like a great idea, as I would be too busy to juggle the home repairs by myself while attempting to teach for the first time.

Homeschooling seemed overwhelming to me prior to this scenario, but considering the reality of the coming months, I was really unsure how we would be able to manage. Though neither of us could act as the GC, there were many appointments and decisions which had to be made about the home throughout the entire process.

Our general contractor drew up an estimate and handed it to us. Typical of most estimates, it was so much more than we had thought or perhaps hoped it would be. For the next few weeks, we spent time slicing and dicing the scope of work to include that which we felt was necessary in order to bring the cost down. We even decided to cut demolition costs some by doing a little bit ourselves. Was that ever a stress release! By that point, the house wasn't looking so sweet to us anymore, so taking axes and hammers to it was actually quite fun. Finally, we came to an agreement and the 'cavalry rode in' with dump trucks.

The contractors began renovations while we were getting accustomed to our new work and homeschool routines. On a daily basis, we would ride over to pick up the mail and check on the house. There was a lot of progress made early on, but then for a long time when it seemed like no one was doing anything to help the cause, feelings of frustration grew. This, too, was yet another lesson in patience and trust when we had no control over the slow progress.

But God was always in control. Besides, we had all kinds of other tasks to occupy our time, like home schooling and choosing paint colors, cabinet styles, faucets, windows, countertops, etc. Mike and I were responsible for fixing some things back at the house in our "spare" time, such as painting molding, pulling up old tile flooring, or re-directing electrical wires. And, with the boys playing soccer, we were running in many different directions.

Through the *Classical Conversations* home-school program and our new church, we met wonderful Christian friends who embraced us with open arms the very week we arrived. Our new friends rallied behind us to help with teaching the boys when I couldn't, inviting us for Bible study and meals, eventually helping us move our large furniture into our home and so much more.

I should go no further without giving recognition to Mike's parents for so graciously loaning us a large sum of interest-free money to pay our contractor. We are forever grateful for their generosity and love. Likewise, we thank my Mom, for flying out to help with painting several rooms. The prayers and support of all of our family and friends was profoundly appreciated.

Living Thin

Life without our 'stuff' was both strange and simple. There were times when we would think something buried in the storage facility would come in handy, but then other times it seemed we could enjoy one another more fully without the distractions of unnecessary 'necessities.'

Never before had I paid so much attention to cans with pop-lids that didn't require a can opener. We also realized that eating off of plastic-ware long-term really ruins the party-like feel. Our small, shaky card table became the meeting place for breakfast, lunch, dinner, and schoolwork. When human leg suddenly met table leg, we had drinks splashing all around us. There were a lot of memories made around that table and whether good or bad, we cherish each one.

The weather was ferociously hot, and without a freezer, cold water was not easy to come by. If we failed to stock the water in our tiny little fridge the night before, we were drinking water at room temperature at the soccer field. Those months reminded us to be content with what a large part of the world goes without every day, like food in our bellies, a warm and safe place to sleep, clothes on our backs and healthy bodies.

However, this did not remedy the stark reality of the differences in comfort level from the life we left behind to the one we were now living. Our oldest son Samuel said, "We went from living in the Golden Ages to the Dark Ages." One month we were drinking wine in bottles and the next month wine in boxes. So much had changed for us!

The climate was also drastically different, moving from what felt like a humid steam room in Houston to a dry sauna in Central Texas. The air in Houston was always full of water. You could practically stick out your tongue for a drink, and now we were living in near-desert conditions. Even the lizards and spiders were different. Oh my goodness, the gargantuan spiders were about four-times the size as the ones I was used to. I'm not normally afraid of spiders, but I was terrified of these.

It was rather difficult not to question what we had done to ourselves and why we willingly chose to change jobs and move locations. Of course, we knew all of the reasons, but they weren't easing our regrets at all. At the end of the day, it came down to resting in our Sovereign God with the assurance that though we make our plans, He orders our steps (Proverbs 16:9).

Nearing Home

By late October, we were nearing the end of our lease and so we continued to check in with our contractor on the estimated date of completion. He wasn't sensing the urgency as much as we would have liked and there were still quite a few loose ends. Days before we were due to move in, we had to get into the house to start cleaning it ourselves. Since the crew hadn't made much headway in that department, the house still looked filthy.

When lamenting to myself one day about all of the disappointments and frustrations with our workers, I was gently reminded that we were paying imperfect people to fix up an imperfect house in an imperfect world. Certainly, we would get imperfect results! How could I have anticipated anything different? No amount of money, no matter how much we were paying, could impact that cold, hard truth. Keeping a close reign on my expectations was important. I had an altered view after that.

Thanks to the combined efforts of family and friends, we were able to move into our home the first week of November. Mike and I made numerous trips to the storage facility to transport a few hundred boxes using their complimentary truck. Then, a few men from church assisted in moving the larger pieces of furniture. Oh, how incredible it felt to sleep in a real bed after nearly three months on air mattresses! That was a glorious moment.

As is required with any move, it took time to set up our stuff and find places for everything. Eventually, boxes disappeared and we began to feel somewhat normal again. Mike's parents then returned a few weeks later for Thanksgiving weekend. It was a fabulous weekend to ponder our many blessings, as more surprises lurked around the corner.

Something Stinks

It's never good when your husband approaches you and says, "Can I speak with you in the other room?" On Thanksgiving weekend, Mike did just that, and for a moment I actually did not want to leave the kitchen. He walked me into our boy's room and asked if I smelled a moldy, musty smell. Leaning in their closet, I sniffed an offensive odor that had not been there previously. There were no visible signs of moisture, yet it was clear that something in our newly renovated house was not right.

This began a three-month quest to discover what was causing this abnormal 'wet basement' smell, in a house built on a slab. We also noticed a foul smell in the hallway closet not too far from their bedroom. Upon opening that door, you could actually feel the dampness in the air.

Our insurance company sent out an adjuster to investigate. She was a very cooperative woman who did her best to figure out the source of the problem. After a few visits, the first plumbing company determined that our sewer pipes were old and cracked and that we needed a whole new sewer system. The insurance company wasn't too fond of that recommendation and called in another company for a second opinion. All investigative testing costs were covered by our insurance, which was of major benefit to us since the tests themselves are not cheap.

This second company wasn't too reliable, but did locate by camera one four-foot segment of pipe that was cracked and needed replacing. Our deductible had not, to date, been met, making us responsible to pay for the repair. Once that section was fixed, our adjuster was ready to close our claim, but we were not convinced that the root cause of the moisture in our home was remedied.

The first plumber had performed a hydrostatic test, the 'second opinion plumber' had not. We felt strongly that, in order to accurately compare reports, a second hydrostatic test was necessary. Thankfully, our adjuster agreed to pay for that test as a last ditch effort to finalize our claim. We prayed for revelation of what was happening under the house, which their cameras don't always show.

The second hydrostatic test failed miserably, leading the experts to the conclusion that there must be multiple cracks and holes in the piping. Authorization was then granted to go ahead with an entirely new sewer system, courtesy of our insurance company. What a miracle in the current economy, considering the pipes were damaged by age only! With the $50,000 we had just unexpectedly spent on the renovations, there would have been no way to come up with more money on our own. Though it was a tough process, God eventually provided $28,000 worth of insurance funds for a brand new system, along with some extra to cover cosmetic repairs.

> The life span of underground cast iron pipes is about fifty years.

Installing new lines outside through the yard is a dirty, nasty job, but one that will reap lasting benefits. Naturally, a normal house inspection would not have detected bad cast iron pipes. However, with a sixty year old house, it would have been smart to have those pipes checked *prior* to buying. The life span of underground cast iron pipes is about fifty years.

Recent events have forced me to recognize that everything has a life span. I just haven't given it too much thought until now. Not only had our pipes reached their max, but our five-foot stone wall along the perimeter of our backyard had seen better days as well. This wall was built the same time our stone house was built sixty years ago. Being a part of the initial attraction to the home, it gave the yard a beautiful "English Garden" feel.

They All Came Tumbling Down

One morning, about two months after we moved in, I was on my way out the door to take the boys to school (we re-organized our educational plans after three months of homeschooling), when I glanced out the window to see what I thought was a hallucination. With a bit of lingering morning darkness, I had to do a double take, but I said to myself, "Why am I not seeing our stone wall?"

After wiping the sleep out of my eyes and taking another few looks, sure enough, I determined half of the wall truly was missing and was lying in our neighbor's driveway. "Classic," was one of the first thoughts that came to my mind and I began laughing heartily. The looks on Samuel and Hudson's faces were priceless, as they weren't sure if they should be thinking it was humorous or not.

It just struck me so funny that such a thing would happen with all that had gone on since we bought the crazy house. The Bible verse, "A merry heart doeth good like a medicine" (Proverbs 17:22a KJV) was certainly applicable in that moment. Since my only two options were either to laugh or cry, by this point in our journey, I couldn't help but laugh.

That very morning, for the first time ever, Mike was going to have to fire someone who started the job the same time he did. As much as I wanted to share the drama of the vanishing wall with my husband, I had to wait until later that day to inform him. I quickly took one son to school, the other to the dentist, and then returned home to begin making phone calls to masons.

Thankfully the neighbors were not parked in the driveway when the wall fell, which must have been the night before when we weren't home. I was told that the weight of those walls falling makes for a very loud crash, which we certainly never heard.

Literally, tons of limestone was covering the ground and, by late that afternoon when Mike returned home, we all pitched in to move it off of the neighbor's property. Only Mike could move the stones that were approximately 100 lbs. each, but the rest of us did what we could. I discovered the repairs would *not* be covered by our insurance, which was probably best since we were already tapping them out with our pipes. Our adjuster didn't seem moved to compassion when I explained our situation and inquired about possible coverage.

Ultimately, the wall fell due to moist soil from heavy rains that had recently saturated the ground, along with the added pressure of an inconspicuous leaning tree limb. Rebuilding the wall to its original state would be too expensive, and the integrity of the remaining wall had been compromised. Thus, it was a judgment call on our part to decide how to proceed.

Being the Mr. Fix-It/Handy Man that my husband is, Mike decided we would rebuild what we could with mortar, a level, and some teamwork. On the warmer weekends, we were adding a layer at a time back to what was left of the wall. It took 18 months to rebuild 159 linear feet of wall to fully complete the "Nehemiah Project," as we sometimes refer to it, and still the wall will never be the five feet it once was. The new height is now three-plus feet. We will always be grateful to Mike's family for helping us work on the wall when they would come to visit.

The wall falling is just another facet of our story. I now realize the importance of seeking something positive in all circumstances, especially if my challenges will draw me closer to the Lord. I confess, this is much more difficult to put into practice through the storms of life, but now more than ever, I know it's true.

Timely Tips for Buying an Older Home

Practically speaking, I would not recommend purchasing a home in a single weekend if it's at all avoidable. Here's a quick list of things we learned:

- ❖ There are many quirks about homes, especially older homes, which cannot usually be detected in just two showings. Had we not been pressed for time, we might have seen more red flags that originally went unnoticed.

- ❖ Do not buy a home with lead-based paint that is in bad shape, *unless* you can either make the necessary repairs on your own, or have the resources to pay a *certified* painter.

- ❖ Before buying, always count the cost of repairs. The final price tag will be higher than anticipated, either due to labor costs or the ever-increasing cost of materials in the current global financial crisis.

- ❖ Hire a reputable home inspector. Interview several and get referrals before choosing the one you will trust. Don't simply contract the first one on your realtor list.

- ❖ When possible, act as your own General Contractor. They tack on a lot of extra fees, and it is rare to find a quality company to manage the various parties involved. Get every single detail *in writing*. (There are crucial discussions containing agreements between you and your contractors that can be easily forgotten.)

❖ Of great concern in any older home is plumbing (both supply and sewer lines), electrical wiring, windows, overall condition of paint and the status of the kitchens and bathrooms.

❖ A fresh coat of paint does not fix every problem!

As stated earlier, everything will eventually come to the end of its life. Therefore, be sure to properly assess what is in the home, how long it has been there and when it will quit. If it's been functional for fifty years or more, assume it will likely soon need to be replaced. A house is like an onion with layer upon layer. The more you peel back, more is revealed.

Personal example: only when our kitchen was gutted did we see there was no insulation in the wall. That was an eye-opener. It is best to reasonably expose as much as possible before taking ownership. Don't worry about what sellers, realtors, or anyone thinks about your attention to detail. You may irritate or offend some folks in the process, but it is worth the peace of mind in the end. Finally, the utmost priority when buying a home is to *pray hard*.

Sometimes in life, you don't get to choose the outcome of your decisions. Certainly you pray, as we had done, but the results aren't always what you think. Just because our walk has been arduous doesn't mean it was the wrong road to take. I can't even begin to fathom all the "whys" to what has transpired, but I am confident that the Lord has those answers. My job is not to figure out every reason why, but to worship Him all the more through the unanswered questions. That is when we reveal our true heart of praise to the Father. It's so easy to praise Him when all is well and life makes sense, but love often grows out of difficulty, stress, confusion and tumult.

This move was worthwhile because it allowed us the opportunity to renew our sense of dependence upon God. Prior to this, we had placed a lot of our security and reliance in our bank account. While we were mindful that God provided our funds, it was still so easy to rely on the gift rather than the Giver.

Immediately upon moving, it became clear that with our dwindling bank stash, our only source of comfort could be found in Christ. We cannot afford to focus on what we have, but can only afford to trust in our Source. We gained a new perspective on the significant difference between what we have and who it comes from.

I remember a dinner that Mike and I shared in Houston at a swanky restaurant. It was our 'favorite place' for special occasions, but I can distinctly recall mentioning to him my feeling that the plentiful times wouldn't last forever. I had a certain awareness that we might as well enjoy those moments because soon enough we wouldn't have the same degree of supply. Yet, I wasn't prepared for the impact that would have upon my faith. Initially my faith was weakened, but it gradually strengthened over time.

It was fear that caused me to doubt God's involvement in our purchase, but then I witnessed His active role in each episode we encountered. We received the blessing of watching Him divinely rescue and deliver us from adversity.

If we never have calamities, we'd have no need for God's extraordinary interventions. What a shame it would have been to have missed all that He has done for us since our move. The headaches are but a small price to pay in exchange for the incredible reward of catching those glimpses of our Creator. Our path has humbled us with the sobering fact that although everything in life fails, including our own plans, He never will.

> *Many are the plans in a person's heart, but it is*
> *the Lord's purpose that prevails.*
> Proverbs 19:21

Since the purchase of this unusual home, we have been to Colombia, South America to adopt our little two-year-old daughter, Sofia. She is charming, independent and beautiful; an amazing addition to our family. When we originally submitted our paperwork to the adoption agency, we were told there would be a two-year wait. That wait turned into five years, but Sofia was "worth the wait"!

Less than two years into his job, Mike's company promoted him to a Regional Manager position which required a future relocation to New Jersey. After less than three years in Temple, our newly renovated home went on the market. Our first and final offer came six months later.

After 13 showings and no offers, I asked the Lord to please not send any people to only look at our house. Because I was homeschooling with three children and Mike was often working from home, it was so challenging to have to get our house into 'inspection mode,' often with little notice. Several times I asked Him to send no one else until He was ready to send *the* buyer. For several weeks no one came and I wondered why, but then remembered my simple prayer request.

Then on a Tuesday we got a call for a Wednesday showing and another call for a Thursday showing for the same couple who wanted to return for a second look. By Friday we had a good offer on the table, but getting to the final sale would prove to be a roller coaster ride as even the sales contract on our house was fraught with drama.

Then after coming to an acceptable agreement with our Buyers, they backed out of the deal the day before the 14 day grace period ended. Hours after signing the cancellation papers, our Buyer while driving on a major highway pulled over to the shoulder to stop and help an elderly man change a flat tire. Before he even got out of his car, he sadly witnessed the car behind him swerve too close to the shoulder and hit the older man who died from the impact.

Seeing someone die in an accident right before your eyes and realizing it could have been you is terrifying. Needless to say our Buyer was very shook up over the incident. We soon learned that the accident was a factor in the Buyer's reconsideration of their decision to cancel the contract on our home.

The next morning, our Buyers asked us for an extension over the Memorial Day weekend to rethink their decision. Again we were hopeful. Monday came and they told their realtor that they were *not* going to buy our house after all. What an emotional time!

Then two days later, the Buyers sent us an email via their realtor saying that they *were* still interested in our house. They requested that we prayerfully consider taking $14,000 less than our agreed upon price! By this time we were really frustrated but decided to make a counter offer for $4,000 less than our original contract agreement. We also requested additional non-refundable earnest money. They agreed to our terms and we had a new contract.

Until the day of the closing, we prayed hard that nothing would go wrong in the last minute. Though the closing date was changed more than once, ultimately the house did sell. We took with us the many lessons learned in that chapter of our lives and moved forward with spirits of anticipation, while grateful for the 'character building' experience in Temple, Texas.

LAKESIDE VIEW

Chapter Eleven

Our "Little Island" Property

My people will live in peaceful dwelling places,
in secure homes, in undisturbed places of rest"
Isaiah 32:18

*B*ack in October of 2007 when I found the short sale, it sounded too good to be true. The online listing described the 3800-square-foot house location as "on an island" on Lake Murray. Property history showed the original asking price had been $839,000; was then reduced to $799,000, then $649,000, and when we found it, the new number was $599,000. The notes indicated that there were water views from every room in the house. The prospect of owning such a place made us more excited than we had ever been about a listing.

We asked our realtors, Barbara Scott and Denise Johnson of Coldwell Banker in Irmo, to check out the property for us and email additional photographs. The house description seemed perfect, but it would be another week before I would be able to get back to South Carolina. Joey and Nicole were about to have a baby and I promised to help, remaining on 'high alert' waiting for the phone call. Little Dominick was born on October 14 and I left for South Carolina within days.

While I was in Lexington helping Nicole and Joey, I made an appointment to see the short sale house with Denise. The day before getting inside, Joey and Nicole came with me to do a 'drive-by', as I hoped that we might meet a neighbor or two. I could not imagine living on an island if the neighbors were not nice. Surrounded by water, my first drive across the one-lane causeway was impressive. Once on the island, it didn't take long to locate the property. As God would have it, a resident on the island was outside working in her front yard and we introduced ourselves. These wonderful folks were the first homeowners on the 'Little Island,' the unofficial name of the 12 lots grouped together on the west side of the causeway. They were warm and welcoming and a wealth of information that Sunday and have been ever since. They were neighbors who became friends.

Confident that we found a wonderful neighborhood, I anxiously anticipated our appointment with Denise the next morning.

The Interior Tour

The front of the all-brick house was deceiving. The house did not look very large, but once inside, there was a real spatial 'wow factor.' As is often the case, the house was more spectacular than the pictures portrayed and I could not believe the view when I walked into the foyer. The two-story foyer with a balcony/ loft above was defined by three arches with fluted columns on a hardwood floor. Looking straight ahead, I could see wide water views of the lake through a wall of floor to ceiling casement windows. In those first few moments, I knew that I wanted to buy this house.

The staircase to the second floor hugged the wall to the right of that massive room, where an arched opening with wood molding led to a sunken living room that ran the depth of the house. Sliding glass doors led out to a screened porch with the same amazing views of the lake. Adjoining the living room with stone fireplace was a huge guest suite with 13-foot ceilings, a large walk-in closet and a tiled bath with marble floors.

Our new friends on the island revealed that the original owners built that side of the house for their parents. In the family room, on one wall was a massive solid oak built-in entertainment unit, and on the opposite, a built-in wet bar with space for an under-counter refrigerator.

After touring the southern side of the house, we turned to the north side to see the dining room, eat-in kitchen, powder and laundry rooms. The pickled oak kitchen cabinets, though most popular in the late 80's and early 90's, are still available today, so I thought they might not need to be replaced. It was obvious that the massive island with cooktop needed a facelift to include a more contemporary appliance and the removal of a tile top. The plain grey Formica countertops would also need replacing.

The dining area of the kitchen and the back wall of the dining room, had the same massive bank of casement windows as the living room, with picturesque views of a lovely back yard and, of course, the lake. Old oak trees, young crepe myrtles, azalea bushes, a grand deck and a covered dock at the water's edge, added to the glorious view.

The powder room was small, but dramatic with a black marble floor and a black toilet. Above the two-car garage was a spacious bonus room, pre-wired for all kinds of electronics. Clearly it would make a perfect office. The tour being half over, I couldn't imagine anything other than that the upstairs bedroom arrangement would work for our circumstances as well.

At the top of the open staircase, we turned to the left into a huge loft, the size of a large bedroom. Once in the loft, facing the front of the house, to the right is the master suite and to the left a guest suite. There is a separate door to the hallway of the guest suite of two bedrooms with a Jack and Jill bath. It could be a perfect bedroom arrangement for Sean and Tyler.

The master suite on the opposite side of the house did not disappoint. The large bedroom had sliding glass doors leading out to a large balcony overlooking the lake. A corner fireplace added warm ambiance.

The back wall of the master bathroom boasted a large bank of casement windows overlooking the lake above a cultured marble, jetted tub. Though I wanted to someday update the master bathroom, I knew immediately that I would never want to replace the marble rust-tone floor.

We ended the tour back outside on the dock, taking it all in. "Lake Murray, created by The Dreher Shoals Dam, is 41 miles long and about 14 miles at its widest point. The area covered by water is about 48,000 acres. Lake Murray, with 640 miles of shoreline, is, at its deepest point near the intake towers, 180 feet. When the dam was built between 1927 and 1930, it was the world's largest earthen dam, but is now surpassed by Brazil and Egypt.

> **Short Sale Note:**
>
> A short sale is different from a foreclosure, because the sellers still own the property. However, since they owe more than the market value of the house, the bank must agree to the price of the sale as well.

Due to earthquake concerns, with the potential to flood Columbia, a new stone and concrete dam was constructed immediately downstream of the original dam." (www.lakemurray-sc.com) Looking north to south, and east to west, I could see water everywhere. I could hardly wait to call Keith and share my excitement.

Negotiations

Not wanting to lose the opportunity to buy this property, we decided to make an offer, subject to Keith's property inspection in the immediate future. Our prayer was that we would not end up in a bidding war over this incredible find. Knowing how long it takes to hear back from banks in short sale and foreclosure negotiations, we wanted to move forward as quickly as possible.

A short sale is different from a foreclosure, because the sellers still own the property. However, since they owe more than the market value of the house, the bank must agree to the price of the sale as well. The banks are taking the loss; therefore, bank representatives are essentially the decision makers. With our initial offer of $500,000, the wait began.

After I returned to Delaware, Keith and I arranged a trip to South Carolina so that he could see the house and give the final approval to satisfy the terms of our contract. Needless to say, Keith was very impressed and our "subject to inspection" clause was then eliminated from the contract. We returned home to prepare for a potential move and to wait to hear back from the bank.

For some reason the bank, located in California, could not figure out the true value of the property. More than 30 days later, their initial response was not a counter offer but a "Give us a different number." response. Keith never wants to "negotiate with himself," but since we had already been waiting a long time, it was clear we would need to play the game their way. I strongly encouraged Keith to make an exception for this house as my heart was set on living there.

My thought was that maybe we could meet the bank half-way and offer an additional $50,000, which Keith felt was too much. He did agree to go back to the bank with an offer of $525,000. We waited a few more weeks for the bank's response.

By the end of November, the sellers and the bank agreed to our second offer and a closing date of December 28, 2007. To say that we were excited is an understatement. One of the most amazing aspects of acquiring this property is that the Lord protected it for us, as there were no other interested buyers bidding simultaneously. We were the only buyers with a contract. What a blessing!

Title Issues

The day after Christmas, we left for South Carolina to close on our house. While driving through Virginia, Denise called to tell us that there was a problem with our title work. Our attorney informed her that we might not be able to close on time. She thought we might want to turn around and go back to Delaware. We opted to keep going believing that somehow it would all work out, but what we did not know was the extent of the title issue.

Our Columbia attorney, Rex Casterline, is a man with focused attention to detail. Essentially the problem was that when Rex looked for the owner of the causeway there was no one to be found in any of the records. In the 60's, our island was sold for $1.00, but it was the Buyer's responsibility to 'build' a road the short distance from the mainland to the island.

No permit was required in those days, and therefore no record of a permit application could be located by our top-notch title company. The causeway was built by the original owner of the island, but it appeared that now, almost 40 years later, we had no way to get legal documentation for a 'right of way' to our property. Rex clearly needed more time.

When we arrived in town, we spent a night in a hotel and went on to spend time with our friends the Baldwin's in Lincolnton GA, a little over an hour from the island. From there we visited our friends the Whittles in Summerville.

Back in Lexington, we got a hotel room again and asked Denise to show us other homes, just in case the lake house deal fell apart. It seemed prudent to have a back-up plan, but we really thought the title work issue on the island would work out within days. When it didn't happen, we headed north wondering if our dream to live on the lake might fall apart.

While we were house hunting in Lexington, we got an offer on The Villa in Delaware, and via fax machines, ended up with a solid contract. That was a huge relief as we didn't want to leave The Villa vacant while moving to South Carolina. Now that we knew we would have to be out by January 31, I felt pressured to come up with an acceptable "Plan B" in South Carolina, however Keith did not share my concern.

Rex could not give us any indication of how long it would take to finish the title work, but he thought it could still be weeks, maybe months. Nor was he able to assure us that there was an acceptable solution. I was adamant that I did not want to have to move twice.

Being far more patient than I, Keith thought it would be worth the hassle to move twice if it meant we would end up on the lake. He gently persuaded me to his way of thinking on the trip back to Delaware. By the time we got home, I was immediately on the computer looking for a short-term rental in Lexington.

Double Move

Short term rentals are sparse, but I did find a two-story, three bedroom, two-and-a-half bath, unfurnished house for $1200 per month in Lexington. It was newer construction, with a two-car garage, a fenced yard and a gas fireplace. Trusting Denise's judgment, we asked her to check it out for us. She said it was perfect for our needs. We signed a three-month lease, with an option for month-to-month thereafter, and moved in on February 1, 2008.

To minimize the stress of a double move, while we were packing at The Villa, we labeled everything with either a G or an H so that the movers would know what to store in the garage and what would be needed in the house. Determined to basically 'camp out' in the rental, we were living with only the bare essentials in the house.

Our living room and dining room furniture, guest room, mirrors, pictures and hundreds of boxes snugly fit in the two car garage that we were using for storage. Keith continued to work on finding a company to purchase, Sean got a job as a trainer in a local computer school, Ty went to daycare and I managed the 'campground'.

We continued to hope for a resolution on the lake house so that we could get in to prepare the walls and floors for the major move.

Occasionally, we would ask Denise to show us a property that could be a substitute if needed. Until Rex could give us something definitive, all we could do was wait and pray. Time seemed to stand still while we waited.

Three months passed. Shortly after the month-to-month clause kicked in on our lease, we got a call from Rex indicating that the causeway issue had been resolved. He arranged for the seller's title company to give us title insurance. (That title company had not done their homework when they issued title insurance to our Sellers. Their initial incompetence had them backed up against a wall.) We also got a letter from the son of the woman who originally owned the island, giving us right-of-way onto the island via the causeway.

With a date of May 5, 2008 for our closing, we were genuinely excited and could begin making plans to get in to paint, replace carpeting, get the water tested and give the house a good cleaning. According to our neighbors, the house had been uninhabited for over two years, as evidenced by the over-grown yard sorely needing attention.

On one of our trips to the lake we pulled up to the house and the entire front yard had been manicured. When inquiring, we were told that one of our neighbors, a retired general, mowed the lawn and cleaned the flower beds as a 'welcome to the neighborhood' gift. This is especially significant since the yard had not been tended to for a very long time. We were so amazed that a Four Star General was so humble to offer such an act of kindness. He and his family also became friends. All of our neighbors were welcoming, and anxious for us to move in. The Southern hospitality on our island was a strong indication that we were going to be very happy in our new home.

> Long before we knew this house existed, God heard our prayers, and was working on our behalf.

Background

The people from whom we purchased the short sale were investors from Florida who bought at the height of the market, paying $700,000 in 2006. Our new friends next door, who are always sharing their tools and flowers with us, thought that about $40,000 had been invested in the property for painting the entire house interior, adding the screen porches and on major dock repairs.

Because some of the carpeting was worn and stained, it was clear that the investors ran out of money before attempting to 'flip' (meaning that they would buy, fix and resell as investors, not residents) the house. Initially, the Floridians tried to resell the property for $839,000, but the market softened and the house did not sell as they had hoped. Even with multiple price drops, the house sat. It is my firm belief that the Lord was preparing and saving this house for us. Long before we knew this house existed, God heard our prayers, and was working on our behalf.

> *Before they call, I will answer; while they are still*
> *speaking, I will hear.*
> Isaiah 65:24

The move to the lake took place in two segments. The first day we had the movers take everything out of the rental house and set it up so that we could sleep in our new house. The next day, June 7, 2008 they emptied the rest of our belongings from the garage to complete our move. We continue to reside in this wonderful space surrounded by tranquility, wonderful neighbors, an amazing State, all while we enjoy everything else about living in the South.

My Mother

In the summer of 2009, my mother's doctor at *Sunrise* had a conversation with my brother, Kurt. The doctor wanted to inform us that my mother's health was declining as she was in the fourth stage of dementia and was losing weight rapidly. Dr "K" warned that most patients in Mom's condition would not last a year. Thinking that Mom might not live much longer, Keith and I decided that we wanted to bring her to our guest suite on the lake until the Lord would call her to her heavenly home. The prices at *Sunrise* were going up and I was sure that I could find a full time home-health aide for less money.

That October, we went out to St. Louis to celebrate Mom's 85th birthday with our family and Aunt Ruth, Mom's sister. The plan was to drive Mom back to South Carolina with us in the spacious Buick Century that Keith inherited from his Mom Emma who had passed away in June of that year. When we bought the lake house, we thought that one day Emma might come to live with us. She consistently resisted our invitations.

In May, Emma came to South Carolina to celebrate her 85th birthday, and the morning after her party, she broke her hip and fell, apparently in that order. While in rehab after hip surgery, Emma's only kidney went into renal failure and, within a week, we lost her. Emma was buried on June 12, 2009 in Belle Haven, Virginia.

My mother handled the trip from St. Louis to Gilbert really well. She seemed happy to think that she was coming to live with us. Mom always had a great relationship with Keith. Once she lost cognitive thought, she rarely called him by his right name; sometimes he would be Ray, Cliff, Hans, and sometimes Tom, probably thinking Tom and I were still married. Thankfully Keith never got his feelings hurt, but always found Mom's name choices amusing, and he would always answer to whatever she called him.

On *Craig's List*, I found a wonderful caretaker, also named Linda, who turned out to be very conscientious and loving towards my mom. Linda, along with the helpful ladies from Hospice, served our family well for the four months that Mom was with us. It was so wonderful to be able to afford for Mom to have one-on-one attention for the rest of her days.

We got a hospital bed for the guest room and used a monitor at night. Though Mom had difficulty speaking in sentences, she could remember the words of all the old hymns that she sang most of her life. When putting Mom to bed, we put a CD player in her room so that she could listen and sing the hymns. Though she had her moments, for the most part, Mom was very content and happy.

I remember praying on the way to St. Louis to pick Mom up, "Lord, please let her live long enough for us to be able to get her to South Carolina at least for awhile." I longed for the opportunity to have Mom with us before passing from this world to the next. It had been over five years since she lived with us, and I really did miss her. I am so grateful for her doctor who honestly shared Mom's prognosis so that we could prepare.

In December, my siblings came to South Carolina to visit Mom one more time. One Sunday evening, my brother Glenn and I decided to take her to a Christmas concert at church. We made a memory with Mom that neither of us shall ever forget. She loved the familiar music so much that throughout the production she kept whispering to us, over and over, "Isn't this glorious? Isn't this glorious?" Mom was so precious!

When the concert was over, someone from church asked Mom if she enjoyed the music, she smiled and said, "No." Glenn and I got the biggest kick out of that. I don't think anyone in the building enjoyed that (her final) Christmas concert as much as our Mother.

By February, Mom's condition was deteriorating. She ended up with a bladder infection. Since she was being cared for by a Hospice team from *Ascension House*, they called for an ambulance to take her to their residence quarters for evaluation, instead of taking her to the local hospital. Dr. Gabriel (so appropriately named) was the attending physician. He actually looked like an angel. The doctor was young with smooth-shaven skin and medium length, curly hair. He had a quiet and gentle voice with the bedside manner of an angel.

After analyzing the test results, Dr. Gabriel explained to me that putting Mom on antibiotics might give her a few more days, but she would not get well enough for us to take her home. He said he could keep her comfortable with morphine until she passed away. The morphine would put her in a constant state of sleep. Having a Living Will was important because we knew that Mom did not want to be kept alive artificially. After conferring with my siblings, the decision was made to let Mom go and keep her comfortable with the drugs. That night we had another of our caretakers, Cynthia, stay with her. The next night I slept in her room on an air mattress.

The following morning the doctor told me that Mom would likely die within the next few days. Keith came to *Ascension House* to stay with her so that I could run home and take a shower. I explained what the imminent signs of death would be to Keith before I left. Shortly thereafter, Keith recognizing that the end was near, put the CD player on with the hymns, kissed her on the forehead and held her hand until Mom peacefully passed away.

I was so happy for Keith that he got to be alone with Mom during those special moments. They had a very special son-in-law/mother-in-law relationship. Keith loved my mother as much as his own. When his mother, Emma, passed away, she was in the hospital with a female caretaker we hired to stay with her through the night. Keith didn't have the opportunity to be with his Mom when she passed. God was

> Prayer is the key to making good choices, and effective in keeping us from major mistakes.

gracious and gave him the chance to bless my mother with his presence. For the amazing son-in-law that Keith had been to Mom, both Keith and I were grateful for that wonderful blessing.

And so it was Valentine's Day 2010 that Mom went to be with the Lord she had so faithfully served for many years. My Mom was one of the most loving women I have ever known. For the Lord to symbolically take her home on Valentine's Day was a gift to us all.

Here it is fitting to include a poetic *Thank You* written by my brother Ron that we printed and presented to Mom's caretakers as a token of our appreciation for their kind service.

To: The caretakers who in all kinds of ways have served our Mother, and who have come, in your own way to care for her, this Thank You is for you, from our family, from our hearts. Perhaps it also speaks for other sons and daughters of those you serve....................................The Family of Amy E Lutjens

With Gratitude
You stand in for us there;
Surrogate daughters and sons, you care for our mothers and
fathers
Day in, day out.
In the easy chores of greetings and smiles,
And in their most demanding and intimate needs
–In the ones that strain your affection and patience –
You are there for them,
Day in, day out.
And our parents live by that service rendered,
By that warmth exuded, by that care extended.

But you do it all without our advantage:
You never saw their youthful skill,
The power and glory of their years in prime;
You never saw their beauty or their strength,
Or what they gave to others.
You never saw the great and small triumphs of their work,
Done with their heads, their hands their hearts.
You never saw the mark they made on towns and schools,
On industries, synagogues and churches,

On big families and small needs in neighborhoods.
You never knew the burdens and delights of their hearts,
The things of which they were proud, the things
of which they were ashamed.

You never ate a meal they cooked for you,
Never rode a bike they bought for you,
Never nursed a scratch they kissed for you.
They never calmed your fears,
Threw you a birthday party,
Tucked you in, set you straight.
They never delighted in your triumphs,
Cried tears in your sorrows,
Or walked you down the aisle at your wedding.
You never saw the poise of their elegance,
The discipline of their dignity,
The pain of their sacrifices.
You never marveled at their knowledge,
Mined gold from the treasury of their hard-earned wisdom,
Learned something for yourself from their
failures and mistakes.

Yet you care for them, people you did not know.
Not perfectly you care, but with devotion and humor and cheer
You work at making a home for them,
Slowly filling in the blanks of long lives lost to you,
Whether they always honor you or not,
Whether they remember your kindnesses or forget them,
And you do it, day in, day out.

They are humbled now in their old age,
As God would teach them their need of Him.

But you keep their humbling from being humiliation,
Their lost powers from defining them,
Their loneliness from overwhelming them,
The world from discarding them.

You do a lot for our mothers and fathers,
Day in, day out,
And for that we are deeply grateful
And thank you from the bottom of our hearts.

Please know that when we complain here and there,
It's because, even from a distance, we are trying to care for them;
And though we sometimes forget it in our own busyness,
Their need now is our duty, even as ours once, was theirs.
Their past is our advantage:
We have loved them from childhood for all they've done for us.
Their decline is our grief,
Their losses the slipping away of what had become
precious to us, too.
That's why it's comforting when we see you remembering
That there's still a person in there, and a whole life lived.

Thank you for your care of the one so dear to us, our Mother, who
gave us our life. *

*This copyrighted material used with the kind permission of Ronald
G. Lutjens.

Seasons and Reasons

It is unclear how long the Lord will keep us on our little island.
Now that Sean and Tyler have moved out we are using only a portion

of this house. It just might be time to downsize. Knowing the importance of not holding too tightly to any earthly possessions, we *are* willing to sell this beautiful home.

Since there seems to have been *seasons* and reasons to move on from each property we have owned, we are planning to put our house on the market and see if a buyer comes our way. Houses on the lake can take as long as a year to sell, so we are taking life one day at a time as we continue to enjoy our home. In the meantime, we share this incredible gift with family and friends, while also using it for ministry purposes. Ultimately, we will stay as long as the Lord allows.

Endless Search

This chapter would be incomplete if I did not detail the acquisition of Keith's new business here in South Carolina. As I mentioned earlier, the search for a company to replace *Auto Doctors* began many months before we sold that business. Keith's efforts intensified once he had the contract to sell the service center. What we could not have known at the time was that it would be three years before the Lord would reveal the next phase of Keith's career. Setting our sights southward to a less densely populated area of the country gave us fewer business options than what we had in the Northeast.

Prayer is the key to making good choices and effective in keeping us from major mistakes. That is not to say that we get it right all the time. We are human, and can misinterpret what we think the Lord is telling us. But when God's children beg for mercy and wisdom day after day, He will honor those prayers. Several Bible passages come to mind:

> *If any of you lacks wisdom, he should ask God,*
> *who gives generously to all without finding fault,*
> *and it will be given to him.*
> James 1:5

Ask and it will be given to you; seek and you will find; knock
and the door will be opened to you. For everyone
who asks receives; he who seeks finds; and to him
who knocks, the door will be opened.
Which of you, if his son asks for bread, will give him a stone?
Or if he asks for fish, will give him a snake?
If you then, though you are evil, know how to give good gifts
to your children, how much more will your Father in heaven
give good gifts to those who ask Him!
Matthew 7:7-11

We were confident that God had a plan for our future. We did not want to make a mistake with the money He had entrusted to us. Working with sellers and brokers via meetings and endless phone conversations was time consuming, primarily because we could only focus on one opportunity at a time. It could be weeks of looking at tax returns and business records only to discover the seller was not making as much money as he thought, which would then cause our interest to wane.

While there is no exact science to purchasing an existing business, there are some guidelines that are very helpful to know. Thankfully Keith knew them well, and his knowledge saved us from regretful purchases. One example is the evaluation of the worth of a company. The seller, generally because of emotional ties to his company, sometimes believes what he is selling is worth more than one should pay. Using a generic formula can help both buyer and seller to effectively analyze value.

Accurate records that can be tied back to tax returns, positive growth potential, and company stability all add to the value of a company.

Our dilemma was that halfway through 2008, as the economy was beginning to meltdown; frightened sellers were listing their companies with asking prices based on performance from previous years. Sellers were trying to validate with tax returns that were not reflecting the existing economy. Some brokers were promoting asking prices that were not reflecting current trends downward. Believing that the economy would not turn around quickly, we were not going to pay last year's prices for this year's reality.

> **Valuing a Business:**
>
> **Accurate records that can be tied back to tax returns, positive growth potential, and company stability all add to the value of a company.**

Keith was always willing to offer a fair price, but it would not have been prudent to overpay a seller just because he had an over inflated idea about what his company was worth.

Another huge problem was that the majority of company owners did not have accurate or clean records for their businesses. They often could not prove their bottom line, and they simply wanted us to trust that their information was correct. Keith would often say to the brokers, "If they will lie to the government, why would I not think they are lying to me?" Brokers had no reasonable answers to that question.

Beyond the State

After an exhaustive search of companies in the Columbia area of South Carolina, we determined that maybe we would need to extend the boundaries beyond the immediate area of our home. Since we were unable to find an open door for a company nearby with decent cash flow and good records, we decided to look elsewhere – even though going miles beyond 'local' was not an ideal solution. We expanded our search to multiple companies in North Carolina and Georgia. Because we signed Non-Disclosure Agreements I cannot provide detailed information about our options.

A few times we were tempted to buy a restaurant, even though we tried to avoid them every step of the way. Keith and I believed that we could own a successful eating establishment, but we also know the challenges of that industry and age was not in our favor. Though Sean is young and energetic, as a single dad, working weekends would not have been good for Tyler. Eventually the Lord made it very clear that the food industry was not on His agenda for us.

> **Buyer Beware:**
>
> Because of emotional ties to their company, sellers often believe their business is worth more than their financials reveal.

There were so many times during those years of living off our savings that we wondered why the Lord was being so slow in opening a new door for us. Again, we clung to the promises of God we had been reading in our daily devotional book, *Streams in the Desert*. The June 20 devotional is powerful, especially the following portion:

"When we have doubts or are facing difficulties, when others suggest courses of action that are conflicting, when caution dictates one approach but faith another, we should be still. We should quiet each intruding person, calm ourselves in the sacred stillness of God's presence, study His Word for guidance and with true devotion focus our attention on Him. We should lift our nature into the pure light radiating from His face,

> Christians need to find the balance between being prepared as the wise virgins were in Matthew 25:1-13, and "not worrying about tomorrow" as Jesus states in Matthew 6:34.

having an eagerness to know only what God, our Lord will determine for us. Soon He will reveal by His secret counsel, a distinct and unmistakable sense of His direction.

"It is unwise for a new believer to depend on this approach alone. He should wait for circumstances to also confirm what God is revealing. Yet Christians, who have had many experiences in their walk with Him, know the great value of secret fellowship with the Lord as a means of discerning His will. You must also have the courage to wait in silent expectation, even when every-one around you is insisting on an immediate decision or action. If you will do these things, the will of God will become clear to you."

One day, I was asking the Lord why our search was taking so long. The strong impression I felt as His answer, was that we were experiencing a semi-retirement phase of life. Keith is a borderline workaholic. I knew that once we found the answer for our future, Keith would likely work until the end of his life. We were living on the lake as if we were retired, with freedom for limited travel when necessary and the savings to do so. Friends would come to visit, and both of us were free to entertain. Since the sale of *Auto Doctors* and The Villa, we tried to maintain a frugal lifestyle, while managing the money the Lord has given us. At the same time, we continued to be mindful of giving generously to those in need.

Our plan would have been to maintain the highest levels of our savings as possible, but for whatever His reasons, the Lord had us in a semi-retired state as we had been living off our savings for a long time.

I believe, as Tara previously indicated, that God wants us to trust Him and not find our security in our savings accounts. The lower the monthly balances, the more intense our trust in the Lord becomes. Christians need to find the balance between being prepared as the wise virgins were in Matthew 25:1-13, and "not worrying about tomorrow" as Jesus states in Matthew 6:34. Of this I am sure; the Spirit of God will lead us if we ask. And so we continued to wait on Him.

Finally, the Answer

Thankfully, during our search for a company, Sean was able to continue teaching at the computer school. Occasionally, he would take time-off to meet with potential sellers, but for the most part Keith handled the details and negotiations. When Sean became increasingly dissatisfied with the owners at the school, he started to send out resumes to companies that he either found online, or heard about through the grapevine.

Sean's resume is very impressive for someone in their mid 30s. He not only posses extensive management experience, but has also mastered great people skills. Many resumes went out, but no interviews were offered. By 2010, the economy was so bad that just getting an interview had become problematic, let alone landing a job. Though discouraged, Sean put up with the challenges at work because he was grateful just to have an income.

After negotiations broke down with a local wholesale company, we had another family meeting. Although we had previously determined that we needed to purchase an existing company with good cash flow, the Lord was *not* opening any of those doors for us, so we decided to look into the purchase of a Business-to-Business franchise.

Keith has a friend from Delaware with whom he had done business when owning *Auto Doctors*. As a former client, Keith had been impressed with *Proforma* and its advertising benefits. Jimmy had been making a decent living over the years, so Keith called him for counsel. Jimmy encouraged Keith to seriously pursue the purchase of a *Proforma* franchise.

Shortly after Mom passed away, Keith and I went to a *Proforma Discovery Day* in Atlanta. We were impressed with the business model, the *Proforma* employees and the opportunity to purchase an inexpensive franchise. After much prayer, and a request for God's confirmation, we all were feeling very positive that we should move ahead with the purchase of a *Proforma* franchise.

After *Discovery Day*, Sean learned that he was losing his job at the computer training school. God's timing could not have been more perfect. Keith knew that we needed Sean to help get *Proforma* off the ground. It was clearly a two-person start-up, and Sean had the perfect college education, (a Penn State degree in marketing) work experience and an affable personality for the job. Suddenly Sean had been set free to work with us. That was one aspect of our decision in which we felt the Lord had given us confirmation that *Proforma* was the way for us to go forward. Sean agreed and our purchase was executed.

One of the ways we hope to expand in the future is with the business acquisition of another print or promotional company. Such a purchase would allow us the opportunity to add to the one hundred plus clients that we currently serve.

> **Being the Boss:**
>
> Self-employment is not without risk, and should only be pursued with clear direction and endless research.

Proforma has been growing stronger with every passing month and year. Almost doubling annually, we stand amazed at how quickly our company is growing in a challenging economy. We are confident that we will continue to experience the Lord's sustenance.

Self-employment is not without risk and should only be pursued with clear direction and extensive research. The greater the risk, the greater the reward when things go well. If life is not going as we hoped, we need to have other options and be as prepared for the future as possible. Being proactive and prayerful helps us stay focused on the One who cares for us and guides us through to the end of our lives.

> *Therefore do not worry about tomorrow, for tomorrow will worry about itself. Each day has enough trouble of its own.*
> Matthew 6:34

I realize that the current real estate market is very different from the one Keith and I experienced over the years. Many wonder if it will ever be as lucrative as it has been in the past. Though real estate is cyclical, it could be many years into the future before we see the kind of return on investment witnessed in the first decade of this century. The good news is that the spiritual principals outlined in this book work for the believer in multiple arenas. These concepts are not limited to the world of real estate and can be applied in all walks of life.

As I age, I am very mindful of my own mortality. No one lives on earth forever. Just as the terminally ill see themselves as "dying," so am I. With every day that passes, I come closer to leaving my earthly home and meeting The One who created me. I *know* where I am going when I pass from this life to the next as years of research have given me a clear vision of Heaven. Sharing descriptions of my eternal home in the final chapter is the most appropriate conclusion to *Properties From Our Father*.

> Being proactive and prayerful helps us stay focused on the One who cares for us and guides us through.

For he was looking forward to the city with foundations,
whose architect and builder is God.
Hebrews 11:10

THE ULTIMATE MANSION

Chapter Twelve

THE ULTIMATE PROPERTY: MY ETERNAL HOME

*T*hough I have been blessed to live in multiple 'charming places' here on earth, I am certain that Heaven will surpass them all. This last chapter describes in detail where I will spend the final segment of my eternity. Because, when all my work on earth is accomplished, I will pass from this human existence into an eternal life. Factual stories of people who have survived a Near-Death Experience or NDE (though I am *not* one of them), along with Biblical descriptions, confirm my belief that there is life after death—a real place called Heaven, and its polar opposite, Hell.

Much has been written about both places, and interestingly, those who have "come back" to recount these experiences describe very similar recollections that coincide with the Holy Scriptures. Heaven, the *ultimate* property from our Father and the final focus of this book, *is* our eternal Promised Land. It is *the* 'location, location, location' so often promoted in real estate—a place far superior to any place on earth that we have dubbed 'paradise.'

Over the years, in addition to the Bible, I've read numerous books about Heaven. What amazes me is how each author's account is so much like all the others. The similarities are too consistent to be a coincidence. My hope and prayer is that this limited compilation of real life stories will offer a glimpse of what lies ahead for us when our final destination is Heaven. I have also included the facts given to us in the Bible of how we can be certain of our eternal destiny. Salvation is simple and God clearly states that He wants *all* people to be saved.

Evangelical Christians believe that the entire Bible is the true Word of God. Jesus said, "I am the way, the truth, and the life, no one comes to the Father except through me" (John 14:6). Either Christ really was who He said He was, the Savior of the world, or He was a liar. Even most non-believers do not see Jesus as a liar. He may often be viewed as a good teacher of morals and values, or a prophet, but *not* a liar.

To those who are skeptical, I suggest a book that can help guide an amazing faith journey: *Evidence That Demands a Verdict*, by Josh McDowell. As a college student skeptic, Josh set out to disprove the Jesus story when challenged by Christian friends. After much research he determined that Jesus did in fact rise from the dead. That knowledge led Josh to a personal relationship with his Creator and he found the truth that many seek.

Heaven

For years I was *not* anxious to get to Heaven, though I was confident Heaven was a far better alternative to Hell. Visions of endless singing while donning a white robe, with bothersome wings, seemed to me to be an extremely boring future. Since I am a borderline workaholic, I couldn't fathom an eternal resting place with nothing to do. However, as I began to read about Heaven, I realized that my assumptions were invalid and, over time, my outlook totally changed. While I still possess a zest for life here on earth, I am so looking forward to that day, when I will go to my 'forever home.'

158

Authors Don Piper, Marietta Davis, Rebecca Springer, Betty Malz and Colton Burpo, share a 'heavenly experience,' relating their personal encounters in each of their books. Words quoted from the Bible, along with excerpts from those books, came together for me, giving me a bird's eye view of what I can anticipate on that day when the Lord takes me 'home.' For those who have given little thought to what life after death might be like, the information I have gathered here should be life-changing.

My hope is that those who already believe in Jesus will be encouraged by this smattering of 'heavenly stories' and the authors' abilities to 'return' and share. Bible reading, along with other books, will greatly expand one's personal faith journey. For those who find these accounts difficult to believe, my prayer is that further investigation into the concept of eternal life, and the truths of the Word of God, will result in coming to faith in our living, and loving Lord Jesus Christ.

Don Piper

In January, 1989, Don Piper, from Houston, Texas, was pronounced dead at the scene of a terrible head-on collision with an 18-wheeler. In his book, *90 Minutes in Heaven*, Don said, "In one powerful, overwhelming second I died. . . . In my next moment of awareness, I was standing in heaven."[1] There, his soul would remain for the next 90 minutes. Don shares his 'heavenly experience' in the early chapters of his book, offering us a rare glimpse into the dimensions of God's reality:

"Joy pulsated through me as I looked around, and at that moment became aware of a large crowd of people. They stood in front of a brilliant, ornate, gate. . . . As the crowd rushed toward me, I didn't see Jesus, but I did see people I had known. As they surged toward me, I knew instantly that all of them had died during my

---

1   Don Piper w/Cecil Murphy, 90 Minutes in Heaven (Grand Rapids, MI: Revell, 2004), 20-21.

lifetime. . . . They rushed toward me, and every person was smiling, shouting and praising God . . . intuitively I knew they were my celestial welcoming committee. It was as if they had gathered just outside Heaven's gate, waiting for me."[2]

Don describes the people he met at the gate and his previous relationship with them. He goes on to say:

"Heaven was many things, but without a doubt it was the greatest family reunion of all. Everything I experienced was like a first class buffet for the senses. I had never felt such powerful embraces, or feasted my eyes on such beauty. Heaven's light and texture defy earthly eyes or explanation. Warm radiant light engulfed me. As I looked around, I could hardly grasp the vivid dazzling colors. Every hue and tone surpassed anything I had ever seen."[3]

For those of us who wonder about our loved ones who died in the faith, and have gone before us, the following excerpt is so hopeful:

"It was as if God had removed anything negative or worrisome from my consciousness, and I could only rejoice at being together with those wonderful people. They looked exactly as I once knew them—although they were more radiant and joyful than they had ever been on earth."[4]

In the case of Don's great-grandmother, she was no longer slumped over.

"She stood strong and upright, and the wrinkles had been erased from her face. . . . As I stared at her beaming face, I sensed that age has no

---

2   Ibid., 21-22.

3   Ibid., 25.

4   Ibid., 26.

meaning in Heaven. Age expresses time passing, and there is no time there. . . . all the ravages of living on earth had vanished. Even though some of their features may not have been attractive on earth, in Heaven, every feature was perfect, beautiful, and wonderful to gaze at."[5]

What great news for those of us who struggle with vanity! Piper continues:

"For me, just to reach the gates was amazing. It was a foretaste of joy divine. My words are too feeble to describe what took place[6]. . . . I paused just outside the gate and I could see inside. It was like a city with paved streets. To my amazement, they had been constructed of literal gold . . . Everything I saw was bright, the brightest colors my eyes had ever beheld—so powerful that no earthly human could take in this brilliance.[7]

"I was in Heaven, and ready to go in through the pearlescent gate. . . . I had arrived at a place I wanted to visit for a long time; I lingered to gaze before I continued forward. Then, just as suddenly as I arrived at the gates of Heaven, I left them."[8]

Revell is the publisher of Don's book, which largely describes his journey to recovery. *90 Minutes in Heaven* is also a 'must read' for those who deal with chronic pain.

Marrietta Davis

The mid-nineteenth century account of *The Vision of Marietta Davis* in *Nine Days in Heaven*, describes Heaven similarly to Don Piper's twentieth century experience. According to the book,

---

5   Ibid., 26-27.

6   Ibid., 33.

7   Ibid., 34-35.

8   Ibid., 35-36.

Davis was given a vision of Heaven while she was in some sort of a trance that doctors could not explain. She was in that condition for nine days, during which she had an amazing journey into the worlds beyond planet earth. Davis said:

"There is no simple way on earth to fully describe the things beyond earth. Our words even spoil the beauty and perfection of the heavenly things that are out there.[9]

"The angel spoke. . . . 'When people die, they are taken to the place where they will spend the rest of eternity. However, the destiny of some is enormously different from the destiny of others.' . . . I looked above me and saw a vast shining Heavenly place, brighter by far than the sun at its peak. Dazzling light radiated from it, shooting across the Heavenly skies. I was spellbound and stared in wonder.[10]

"We stopped on a plain filled with trees laden with fruit. We passed beneath their shady branches and I heard birds singing . . . They were the sweetest songs I had ever heard."[11]

Davis recalls more of what the angel said:

"'When redeemed people die, this is the first place they are brought . . . They meet old friends here—those who have preceded them and have advanced spiritually to take on higher tasks. Family members can meet them here and talk with them for the first time.' . . . I saw many, many, happy people moving everywhere through the flowery landscapes.[12]

"They placed me at the feet of the most glorious Being I could ever imagine. A crown of pure light rested on His head, and hair

---

9 Dennis & Nolene Prince. Nine Days in Heaven (Lake Mary, FL: Creation House, 2006), 6.

10 Ibid., 8.

11 Ibid., 10-11.

12 Ibid., 11.

white as snow fell upon His shoulders. No words could begin to describe His splendor.

"An attending angel spoke quietly to me. 'Marietta, this is your Redeemer, He is God. Yet He put aside His divinity and came to earth as a man, and suffered for your sins. He died for you outside the gate of Jerusalem (Hebrews 13:11-12) He died alone just as it was written centuries before.' (Isaiah 63:3)[13]

Davis then shares something I found overwhelmingly similar in many of the books I read about Heaven:

"I was overwhelmed to find myself in the embrace of someone I had loved very dearly on earth. Others had gathered all around me, people I had known and loved on earth, all eager to greet and hug me.[14]

"'So this is Heaven!' I cried! 'And look at all these happy people . . . They used to struggle so hard in their old human bodies. Look at their faces now. The glory of this place has made them absolutely radiant! They used to look so worried! And whatever happened to the ravages of old age?'[15]

A man Davis knew from earth who had been old and gray, now looked youthful:

"Gone was the walking stick, the gaunt trembling frame, the grief-worn cheek, the hollow eye, the sick body. In their place were light, health and vigor."[16]

Davis goes on to describe Heaven's architecture:

---

13 Ibid., 14
14 Ibid.
15 Ibid., 15.
16 Ibid., 16.

"We found ourselves on an aerial plain suspended above the lofty dome of the central temple. From here I could see the layout of the great city stretching out on every side. Its beauty was breathtaking.... Spaced at regular intervals were groups of majestic trees with luxuriant clusters of fragrant flowers. Beneath them in the open spaces were tiny garden beds filled with every variety of flower, blossoming shrubs, and vines.[17]

"Fountains of dancing waters caught my eye. Some bubbled up from the green grass to flow with a low and pleasant murmur through marble channels or beds of golden sand. Others gushed up very high, cascading down in streams which fed into basins. Some of these basins looked like diamonds, others like polished silver or the whitest pearl.... Flowing out through the gateway was a river, supplied by the fountains within.[18]

"So the city was divided into one hundred and forty-four great suburbs, or divisions, arranged in increasing degrees of magnificence and beauty.... Each building in the city was extremely large and perfectly integrated with all the others. The entire city gave the impression of being one garden of flowers, one grove of shady trees, one gallery of sculptures, and one sea of fountains.... This was then overarched by a colored sky that bathed every object in it in incredible and ever-changing shades."[19]

Davis's unique experience offers optimism and hope for the amazing beauty that awaits us in Heaven.

Rebecca Springer

As her "life hung in the balance between time and eternity," Rebecca Springer of Kentville, Canada, had a "glorious vision of

---

17   Ibid., 25

18   Ibid., 25-26.

19   Ibid., 26.

Heaven."[20] She was gravely ill when she was blessed with this experience. Upon entering Heaven, Springer notes:

"But, even in the first moment, I observed how perfect each plant and flower was. . . . Each leaf was perfect and smooth and glossy, instead of being rough and course looking. The flowers peeped up from the deep grass, so like velvet. . . . Away, away—far beyond the limit of my vision—stretched this wonderful field of perfect grass and flowers. Out of it grew equally wonderful trees, whose drooping branches were laden with exquisite blossoms and fruits of many kinds."

I found myself thinking of John's vision on the Isle of Patmos and, "the tree of life" that grew in the midst of the garden, bearing "twelve manner of fruits . . . and the leaves of the tree were for the healing of the nations" (Revelation 22:2).[21]

Springer continues:

"Everywhere I looked, I saw, half-hidden by the trees, elegant and beautiful houses of strangely attractive architecture. . . . I caught glimpses of sparkling fountains in many directions, and close to me a placid River flowed with water clear as crystal. The walks that ran in many directions through the grounds appeared to be made of pearl, spotless and pure, bordered on either side by narrow streams of clear water, running over stones of gold. . . . There was no shadow of dust, no taint of decay on fruit or flower. Everything was perfect; everything was pure . . . and not a single blade of grass was any color but the brightest green.[22]

"The houses, as we approached and passed them, seemed wondrously beautiful to me. They were built of the finest marbles and

---

20 Rebecca Springer, Within Heaven's Gates (New Kensington, PA: Whitaker House, 1984), 5.
21 Ibid., 10-11.
22 Ibid., 12.

were encircled by broad verandas. The roofs or domes were supported by either massive or delicate columns.

"Winding steps led down to pearl and golden walks. The style of architecture was unlike anything I had ever seen."[23]

Springer goes on in Chapter Three to describe the reunions with her loved ones who had gone on before her, most importantly her parents:

"There advancing up the long room to meet me, I saw my dear father and mother and with them my youngest sister. With a cry of joy, I flew into my father's outstretched arms and heard his dear, familiar, 'My precious little daughter!'

"'At last, at last!' I cried clinging to him. 'At last I have you again!'

"'At last!' He echoed, with a deep-drawn breath of joy. Then he resigned me to my dear mother and we were soon clasped in each other's embrace. 'My precious mother!' 'My dear, dear child!' we cried simultaneously. . . . Oh, what joy it was! I did not dream that even Heaven could hold such joy.'"[24]

In Chapter Five, Springer shares the joy of seeing her Lord for the first time:

"A radiant glow overspread the wonderful face, which He lifted, looking directly at me. The mist rolled away from before my eyes, and I knew Him! With a low cry of joy and adoration, I threw myself at His feet, bathing them with happy tears. He gently stroked my bowed head for a moment, then, rising, lifted me to His side. 'My Savior—my King!' I whispered, clinging closely to Him.[25]

---

23 Ibid., 16.
24 Ibid., 28-29.
25 Ibid., 43.

"Then He drew me to a seat and conversed with me long and earnestly, unfolding many of the mysteries of the divine life. I hung upon His words. I drank in every tone of His voice. I watched eagerly every line of His beloved face. And I was exalted, uplifted, upborne, beyond the power of words to express. At length, with a divine smile, He arose. 'We will often meet.' He said." [26]

Betty Malz

The City of Tomorrow, the title of Chapter Seven in Betty Malz's book *My Glimpse of Eternity*, vividly describes her life-changing encounter. Readers are drawn into the book from the back cover text:

"At 5:00 on a July morning in 1959, twenty-seven-year-old Betty Malz was pronounced dead. A sheet was pulled over her head. Betty describes her experience on the other side of that dividing line that we call "death," then how she returned to her body on the hospital bed—to the stunned amazement of her grieving father and the hospital personnel." [27]

Malz's experience mirrors those of the aforementioned authors, and leaves her readers with incredible hope:

"The transition was serene and peaceful. I was walking up a beautiful green hill. It was steep, but my leg motion was effortless and a deep ecstasy flooded my body. . . . I was walking on grass, the most vivid shade of green I had ever seen. Each blade was perhaps one inch long, the texture like fine velvet; every blade was vibrant and moving. . . . 'Can this be death?' I wondered. If so, I certainly

---

26 Ibid., 44.

27 Betty Malz, My Glimpse of Eternity (Old Tappan, NJ: Fleming H. Revell Co, 1977), Back Cover.

had nothing to fear. There was no darkness, no uncertainty, only a change in location and a total sense of well-being. All around me was a magnificent deep blue sky, unobscured by clouds. . . . Then I realized I was not walking alone. To the left, and a little behind me strode a tall, masculine looking figure in a robe.[28]

"As we walked together I saw no sun—but light was everywhere. Off to the left there were multicolored flowers blooming. Also trees, shrubs. On the right was a low stone wall. . . . My emotion was a combination of feelings: youth, serenity, fulfillment, health, awareness, tranquility. I felt I had everything I ever wanted to have. I was everything I had ever intended to be. I was arriving at where I had always dreamed of being.[29]

"The angel stepped forward and put the palm of his hand upon a gate which I had not noticed before. About twelve-feet high, the gate was a solid sheet of pearl, with no handles and some lovely scroll work at the top of its Gothic structure. The pearl was translucent so that I could almost, but not quite, see inside. The atmosphere inside was somehow filtered through. My feeling was of ecstatic joy and anticipation at the thought of going inside.

"When the angel stepped forward pressing his palm on the gate, an opening appeared in the center of the pearl panel and slowly widened and deepened as though the translucent material was dissolving. Inside I saw what appeared to be a street of golden color and an overlay of glass or water. The yellow light that appeared was dazzling. There is no way to describe it. I saw no figure, yet I was conscious of a Person. Suddenly I knew the light was Jesus, the Person was Jesus."[30]

Malz ends the chapter describing her 'return' back to her hospital room, where her father stood by her bed too stunned to react.

---

28 Ibid., 84-85.
29 Ibid., 85-86.
30 Ibid., 87-88.

Betty went on to say that God healed her that day, and finishes her book with examples of how her heavenly experience changed her earthly life.

Malz's book is very uplifting, as are the others. Her vivid descriptions, as she remembers them, also give us an amazing array of visuals to encourage us as we look forward to Heaven, and attempt to live in light of eternity.

Colton Burpo

The currently popular *Heaven is for Real*, first published in 2010, gives us a glimpse into eternity from the perspective of young Colton Burpo, as he relates his experience to his father, author and pastor, Todd Burpo. Colton's misdiagnosed appendicitis nearly took his life. While in surgery, Colton had an out-of-body experience which he later described to his parents, in bits and pieces. Todd realized that Colton's experience was so hopeful, he felt compelled to tell his son's story. (Both Todd and Colton were interviewed on multiple national television shows.)

There were events that Colton 'witnessed', that he could not have known about otherwise. For example, looking down from the ceiling in the operating room, with a bird's eye view of the hospital, he saw his Dad in one room praying while his mom was on a cell phone in another room nearby. That is exactly how it was and those scenes were not anything his parents ever mentioned to Colton after the surgery. Previously Sonja, Colton's mom, had a miscarriage. The Burpos never told their young son about that incident. But, when Colton *experienced Heaven*, he met his baby sister. Reverend Burpo describes this incredible revelation:

"One evening in October, I was sitting at the kitchen table working on a sermon. Sonja was around the corner in the living room working on the business books ... Colton ... planted himself directly in front of Sonja.

"'Mommy, I have two sisters,' Colton said. Sonja looked up from her paperwork and shook her head slightly, 'No, you have your sister Cassie, and . . . do you mean your cousin Traci?'

"'No.' Colton clipped off the word adamantly. 'I have two sisters. You had a baby die in your tummy, didn't you?' At that moment time stopped in the Burpo household, and Sonja's eyes grew wide. Just a few seconds before, Colton had been trying unsuccessfully to get his mom to listen to him. Now, even from the kitchen table I could see that he had her undivided attention.

"'Who told you I had a baby die in my tummy?' Sonja said, her tone serious.

"'She did Mommy. She said she died in your tummy.'[31] . . . I knew what my wife had to be feeling. Losing that baby was the most painful event of her life. We had explained it to Cassie; she was older. But, we hadn't told Colton, judging the topic a bit beyond a four-year-old's capacity to understand. . . .

"A bit nervously, Colton slunk back around the couch and faced his mom again. 'It's okay Mommy,' he said. 'She's okay. God adopted her.' . . . Now Colton went on without prompting. 'In Heaven, this little girl ran up to me, and she wouldn't stop hugging me.' . . .

"Sonja's eyes lit up and she asked, 'What was her name? What was the little girl's name?' . . . 'She didn't have a name. You guys didn't name her.' . . . 'You're right Colton.' Sonja said. 'We didn't even know she was a she.'

"Then Colton said something that still rings in my ears. 'Yeah, she said she just can't wait for you and Daddy to get to Heaven.'[32]

This part of the story is amazing to me. There is no way this little boy could have fabricated that experience. I totally believe that it really happened as described in the book, which is more detailed than this excerpt. A story like this one can bring hope

---

31 Todd Burpo with Lynn Vincent. Heaven is for Real (Nashville, TN: Thomas Nelson,2010), 94.

32 Ibid., 95-96.

and encouragement to so many people who have suffered the emotional pain of miscarriages and abortions.

"He [Colton] also saw the gates of heaven, he said:'They were made of gold and there were pearls on them. The heavenly city itself was made of something shinny,'like gold or silver.' The flowers and trees in heaven were 'beautiful,' and there were animals of every kind.'"[33]

Colton saw Heaven much like the Apostle John described it in Revelation 21:18-21 in the Bible:"The wall was made of jasper, and the city of pure gold, as pure as glass. The foundation of the city walls were decorated with every kind of stone. The first foundation was jasper, the second sapphire, the third chalcedony, the fourth emerald, the fifth sardonyx, the sixth carnelian, the seventh chryso-lite, the eighth beryl, the ninth topaz, the tenth chrysoprase, the eleventh jacinth, and the twelfth amethyst. The twelve gates were twelve pearls, each gate made of a single pearl. The great street of the city was pure gold, like transparent glass."

According to Colton, old age is non-existent in heaven. Todd had a photo of his grandfather whom he called "Pop." It was taken when Pop was 61-years-old with white hair and glasses. Colton told Todd that he had seen Pop in Heaven, but when Todd showed Colton that photo, not only didn't he recognize Pop, but he said, 'Dad, nobody's old in heaven,' . . .'And nobody wears glasses.'[34]

Todd decided to get a photo of Pop at a younger age to show Colton. When Colton saw the photo of the younger man, he recognized him immediately—more confirmation that our aging bodies will be transformed into our younger version!

Since initial publication, *Heaven is for Real* has been widely circulated because of its appeal to young and old alike. It is an honest portrayal of eternal life and one of the most hopeful

33 Ibid., 105.
34 Ibid., 121.

books I have ever read and I believe it is now a movie soon to be released.

My Personal Faith Journey

Having had the benefit of growing up in a Christian home, and loving Jesus for as long as I can remember, I have never been afraid to die. My whole life I have been confident that I will go to Heaven.

It's not because of any good things I have done, but it is because I believe by faith that Jesus loved me enough to die for me and then He drew me to Himself. Because of *His* goodness, I will go to Heaven.

> **How do you know when you have done enough good works to get you into heaven?**

In 1 John 5:13, we read, "I write these things to you who believe in the name of the Son of God so that you may *know* that you have eternal life." Generally, people who know Jesus personally feel very confident about going to Heaven. In my experience, people who aren't so sure of their destination are the ones who may believe that their good works will get them over the threshold.

The questions I sometimes ask are, "How do you know when you have done enough good works to get you into Heaven? What barometer do you use to assess that you have totally completed your good works here on earth, well enough to get you through the pearly gates to God?" These are legitimate questions with no real answers.

> **Just like Jesus Christ, we will one day be resurrected!**

Some Simple Facts

Man is in a dilemma because our sins (meaning, going our own way and leaving God out of the picture) separate us from God. Romans 3:23 tells us, "For all have sinned; all fall short of God's glorious standard." Sometimes people think that only the larger offenses like murder, adultery, and cheating fall into the 'sin' category. The truth is that even what we perceive as small offenses are sin. Paul tells us in the same chapter in Romans that, "No one is good—not even one." (Romans 3:10). Since I believe the whole Bible is the divinely inspired Word of God, I take these verses seriously and know them to be true.

The good news is that Jesus Christ came to our rescue! He stepped out of eternity into time to permanently settle the problem of sin. The gruesome death of Jesus Christ took place on our behalf more than 2,000 years ago. He paid for our sins so that we would not have to pay for them ourselves. How amazing is that! Then, He was resurrected from the dead, and walked out of His grave, proving that He is God, just because He loves us so much. And, like Him, we will one day be resurrected.

God offers to give us eternal life *if* we accept His amazing gift of love. "To all who believed and accepted Him, (Jesus) He gave the right to become children of God." (John 1:12) We make the choice to accept or reject God's gift. He promises eternal life, peace of mind, freedom from guilt, and cleansing of all our sins, if we will yield ourselves to Him and His purposes for our lives.

Becoming a Christian is simple, and yet totally life-changing. It is extremely important and often overlooked. Becoming part of God's family simply requires a repentant heart and confession, coupled with a desire to know the truth. Jesus is the Truth. Jesus can be trusted. Jesus has all the answers that we seek. Jesus is The One who saves us from Hell itself.

The alternative to Jesus is eternal separation from God because Jesus is God. As for me, I choose Jesus, and would encourage all skeptics to seek the Truth, and respond to His love.

For those who are ready to choose eternal security, and have not yet made the choice for Christ, all it takes is a repentant heart and the simple prayer of a yielded spirit. A sample prayer:

Lord Jesus,

I admit that I am far from perfect and lack a stellar track record. I am truly sorry for all my actions over time that have offended you. I trust that you will accept me just as I am, with all my faults, failures and fears. I now understand that I cannot save myself and need you in my life. I want to have the confidence that Heaven is a real and an amazing place, an eternal resting place for my soul and resurrected body. Right now I choose you. I want to follow you on the path you have purposed just for me, until I breathe my last breath and I pass from this life into the next. Help me to read your Word and pray so that I may honor you with my life.

Thank you for now making me part of your family of believers. Now I know that I never have to be afraid to die because I know where I am going, and look forward to being with you and my believing loved ones forever. I pray this in your name, Amen

If you prayed that prayer (or a similar one) sincerely, you have received Christ as your Savior. You are a Christian, a new creation (2 Corinthians 5:17), your sins are forgiven (1 John 1:9), you have eternal life (1 John 5:11-12) and Jesus is now living in you (Galatians 2:20).

The best way to grow in your new faith is to pray, read the Bible (God's 'love letter' to mankind) and find a Bible-believing church for fellowship with other believers.

It is amazing just how relevant the Bible is for us today as God speaks to us so clearly from cover-to-cover, Genesis to Revelation. All the Bible stories have meaning for our lives. As we ask God to 'speak' to us through His Word, we end up with a personal relationship with Him.

It is important to note that new believers often do *not* have an emotional experience. We cannot rely on feelings to confirm our decision. It is simply a matter of trusting what the Bible says about Christ. Once we choose Christ, we can *know* that Heaven will be our ultimate destiny.

By sharing the details of God's interventions in my life, hopefully readers have been encouraged to learn that He wants to be just as involved with all people. My prayer is that the essence of this book, and especially this final chapter, has stirred excitement for Heaven in hearts everywhere. My purpose is that all will seriously consider the information I shared and choose to cement eternal destinies in Heaven.

How exciting to imagine that one day we will celebrate eternal life in that Heavenly city, in the 'property' that our Lord has prepared for us. In John 14:2 (KJV) Jesus tells us, "In my Father's house are many mansions: if it were not so, I would have told you. I go to prepare a place for you."

How comforting and exciting to know that He has prepared eternal homes for His people if only we will believe. Sometimes people want to receive Christ into their lives but can't embrace this truth because they have concerns about loved ones who have already passed away who may never have expressed such a belief.

We cannot make personal decisions based on the lives of others. Only God knows who may have turned to Him in their final moments of life. When we get to Heaven we will know the fate of our loved ones, but we should not reject the Lord based on what they may or may not have decided.

Final Note

It would be negligent on my part not to include in this chapter a mention of Hell. The Bible refers to Hell often, and while it may be challenging to imagine that anyone could be damned to such a place of horror, that which we mortals can, or cannot contemplate, does not change the reality. There may be much truth to the saying, "God doesn't damn people to Hell, but people themselves make that choice."

Today most people, even many pastors, avoid the subject because Hell is such a horrific place. Fortunately, the Word of

God warns us of its existence and provides for us a way of escape. As previously stated, while we are on earth, we have opportunities to choose God or reject Him. It is our responsibility to search for the truth so that we will make wise choices about what we believe. Truth is not relative. There is much that is black and white. Very little is gray.

Our culture has obfuscated truth and turned it into, "truth is whatever it is for me." Logic goes out the window and is replaced with, "if it feels good, it must be right." There are many well-intentioned people on their way to an eternity of awful misery because they bought into a pop culture lie.

In addition to books written, there have been multiple TV documentaries of people who experienced an NDE but did not see Heaven, they saw Hell. Thankfully, they were given another chance at life with time to change course and find the Lord. Many of them have reported their journeys to the Truth.

My hope is that readers will reflect on this chapter with an open mind and a heart willing to embrace truth.

If those who believe that Heaven can only be attained by accepting Christ are right, those who disagree and do not act will have *everything to lose*. However, *if* we are wrong, those with differing opinions will lose nothing. Which side of that debate do you think is the safest and most secure? My prayer is that I will meet *all* my readers in Heaven!

Will you be there? I will look for you.

Linda R. Abrams

ABOUT THE AUTHOR

LINDA graduated from *Concordia Junior College (now Concordia University)* in Ann Arbor, Michigan, with an Associate of Arts degree. *Encore,* the Unique Consignment Shop was Linda's first successful entrepreneurial project that opened in Belmar NJ in 1980 and sold for a nice profit three years later. In 1985 she opened *Affordable Interiors by Kristalyn,* an interior decorating company that catered to middle class clients.

Her talents combined with the business acumen of her husband of 20 years, Keith Abrams, made it possible for the Abrams to earn significant income buying and selling real estate. It is their firm belief that God desires to be intricately involved in the details in every arena of their lives.

Linda is the Stonecroft (an international outreach ministry) Regional Administrator for the eastern half of the State of South Carolina. She also serves on the Board of Directors with Designs for Living, a Christian women's ministry in Greenville, SC.

Linda and Keith currently reside on Lake Murray in South Carolina. Together they have five children and nine grandchildren.

Website: LINDAABRAMS.NET
Email: LINDA@LINDAABRAMS.NET

Sandy Huston

About the Artist

Sandy has been a professional artist her entire working career and always looked for venues that were open to her and her talents.

Upon graduating from college with a degree in Fine Art, Sandy began working as a paste-up artist in the advertising department of a local newspaper. From there she worked in a sign painting/silk-screening shop. Learning how to hand-letter and prep art for production proved invaluable to later endeavors.

Sandy participated in several regional and national shows and was accepted in the Pastel Society of America, which led to exhibiting in New York City. There she enjoyed a good deal of success in the sale of her pastel and oil paintings. Raising a family led Sandy away from the city, allowing her to easily obtain work based on past experience with calligraphy, signs, display and portraits.

This segued into mural and decorative painting for several years while teaching at her Manasquan, NJ studio. Sandy was then contracted to illustrate the children's alphabet book, *ABC Shells*. She is now focused on illustrating, portraits and architectural renderings.

Contact information for Sandy Huston on the following page.

Translate the ordinary into the extraordinary!
A Portrait of your Home or Business Could
Become a Family Heirloom

Sandy Huston
732.742.4239
NJMuralsandFaux.com

27489428R00108

Made in the USA
Charleston, SC
13 March 2014